COMBAT LEGEND

Ju 87
STUKA

Robert Jackson

Airlife

First published in the UK in 2004
by Airlife Publishing Ltd, an imprint of the Crowood Press Ltd

Text written by Robert Jackson
Profile illustrations drawn by Dave Windle
Cover painting by Jim Brown – The Art of Aviation Co. Ltd

British Library Cataloguing-in-Publication Data
    A catalogue record for this book
    is available from the British Library

ISBN 1 84037 439 X

Printed in Malaysia

*Contact us for a free catalogue that describes the complete range of Airlife
books for pilots and aviation enthusiasts.*

Airlife
An imprint of The Crowood Press Ltd
Ramsbury, Marlborough, Wiltshire SN8 2HR
E-mail: enquiries@crowood.com

www.crowood.com

Contents

Junkers Ju 87 Timeline   4

Chapter 1   Junkers Ju 87 Stuka: 5
             Prototypes and Development

Chapter 2   Operational History 1939-40:   21
             Blitzkrieg and Battle of Britain

Chapter 3   Operational History 1941-45:   37
             Mediterranean and Eastern Front

Chapter 4   Stuka Men: 61
             Engineers and Aces

Chapter 5   Stuka in Service: 69
             Variants, In Flight and Users

Appendices   1: Specifications   89
             2: Weapons and Systems
             3: Junkers Ju 87 Production
             4: Museum Aircraft and Survivors
             5: Stuka Models
             6: Stuka Books

Index   96

Junkers Ju 87 Timeline

1928
First flight in Sweden of the Junkers K.47 two-seat all-metal fighter monoplane, progenitor of the Stuka.

1934
Mock-up of the Junkers Ju 87 built at Dessau.

January 1935
Reichsluftministerium announces a competition for a new dive bomber (*Sturzkampfflugzeug*, or Stuka).

17 September 1935
First flight of the Junkers Ju 87V-1.

24 January 1936
Ju 87V-1 destroyed in a crash; Ju 87V-2 fitted with redesigned tail unit as a consequence.

March 1936
The Ju 87 is selected as the *Luftwaffe*'s new dive-bomber.

November 1936
Ju 87V-4 delivered to Rechlin for trials.

May 1937
First production Ju 87A-1 aircraft delivered to St.G 162 'Immelmann' (later redesignated StG 2). Total of 27 aircraft delivered by 30 November 1937.

December 1937
Three Ju 87A-1s, known as the *Jolanthekette*, arrive in Spain for evaluation under combat conditions. Flown by relays of St.G 162 pilots attached to the Condor Legion.

June 1938
First Ju 87Bs delivered to the *Luftwaffe*.

October 1938
Five production Ju 87B-1s sent to Spain for combat evaluation.

1939
A small batch of Ju 87C aircraft, intended for service on the German aircraft carrier *Graf Zeppelin*, completed at Dessau.

1 September 1939
Ju 87B Stukas of III/StG 1, Elbing, open the Polish campaign, attacking bridges over the Vistula at Dirschau.

April 1940
One Stuka *gruppe*, I/StG 1, is assigned to the Norwegian campaign. Equipped with long-range Ju 87Rs (Ju 87Bs with auxiliary fuel tanks) it operates from Kiel and Stavanger.

May 1940
Nine Stuka *gruppen* take part in the invasion of France and the Low Countries. Light early losses become substantial when the Ju 87s encounter RAF fighters over Dunkirk.

4-9 July 1940
Heavy attacks by Stukas on Portland and Dover harbours.

13 July 1940
First major sortie by Stukas against a convoy in the English Channel during the preliminary phase of the Battle of Britain.

13–16 August 1940
Thirty seven Ju 87s fail to return from operations over England; many more damaged beyond repair. The Stuka is withdrawn from the battle. I and III/StG 1, II/StG 2 and Stab/StG 3 deployed to the Mediterranean.

February 1941
First appearance of the Ju 87D.

April–May 1941
Three Stuka *gruppen* support German forces in the Balkans and during the invasion of Crete.

22 June 1941
Operation *Barbarossa*, the German invasion of the USSR, is supported by eight Stuka *gruppen* totalling 317 aircraft.

23 September 1941
I and III/StG 2 bomb the Russian Fleet at Kronshtadt. The battleship *Marat* is sunk by *Oblt* Hans-Ulrich Rudel.

June 1942
Ju 87 attacks in North Africa play a major part in breaking the British and Commonwealth defensive line at Gazala.

April–May 1943
After suffering heavy losses in the Tunisian campaign, all surviving Ju 87 units are evacuated from North Africa.

May 1943
Cannon-armed Ju 87G used experimentally on the Eastern Front (in the Crimea) by *Hptm* Hans-Ulrich Rudel.

July 1943
Junkers Ju 87G used with great success against Soviet armour during the battle for the Kursk salient.

October 1943
All Stuka units redesignated *Schlachtgeschwader* (Fighter-Bomber Wings). Specialist night attack Ju 87 units created.

January–June 1944
Progressive re-equipment of Ju 87 units with the Focke-Wulf 190. Specialist antitank units retain the Ju 87G-1 and G-2.

8 May 1945
Oberst Hans-Ulrich Rudel leads the last Ju 87 mission of the war, a sortie against Soviet armour in Czechoslovakia. Afterwards, he leads the remnants of SG 2 (three Ju 87Gs and four Fw 190s) to the American-held airfield at Kitzingen, where their pilots crash-land them.

1. Junkers Ju 87 Stuka: Prototypes and Development

The concept of the *Sturzkampfflugzeug* – literally translated as 'Diving Battle Aircraft' – originated in World War I, when the Germans formed specialist ground attack squadrons units known as *Schlachtstaffeln*. In March 1918, at the time of the Ludendorff Offensive on the Western Front, 27 of these units were operational in support of the various German field armies, and their crews quickly learned that the light bombs carried by their aircraft could be placed more accurately by making a diving attack rather than by releasing them in level flight. Similar tactics were employed by the Royal Flying Corps (which became the Royal Air Force on 1 April 1918) in its maximum-effort attacks on the advancing German columns during this great offensive, which came perilously close to succeeding.

It was to meet the requirement for a dedicated ground attack aircraft that the company established by Hugo Junkers produced the CL.1, which flew in prototype form on 4 March 1918 and which was immediately ordered into production. An all-metal monoplane, it was developed from the early D.I fighter, and like its predecessor it had a skin of corrugated duralumin. Only 47 CL.Is were produced before the end of hostilities, but it was soon apparent that Junkers had produced what was probably the most outstanding assault aircraft of the war.

The construction of the CL.1 and other all-metal designs during World War I gave Hugo Junkers a head start in re-establishing his

aviation concern in the years after World War I, when Article 201 of the Treaty of Versailles forbade Germany to possess or manufacture military aircraft. The embargo was rigidly enforced by an Allied Control Commission, and Junkers sidestepped it by the simple expedient of moving his operations abroad, to Sweden and to the newly-created Soviet Union. In the latter case, Junkers was instrumental in creating a modern aircraft factory at Fili, about 370 km (230 miles) from Moscow, where 350 German aircraft engineers and technicians arrived in October 1922 under conditions of strict secrecy. This clandestine movement of German personnel and equipment to the Soviet Union was the first fruit of secret negotiations which had begun in the spring of 1920 between Leon Trotsky, the Soviet Commissar for war, and General von Seeckt, Commander of the German *Reichswehr*.

New Luftwaffe
The Junkers operation in Sweden, at Malmo-Limhamn, was carried on under the auspices of AB-Flygindustri, with Dipl-Ing Karl Plauth in charge of a small German design team. In its early days the team concentrated on the design of mail aircraft, the A32 and A35, but in 1928 Plauth designed an all-metal fighter monoplane, the K47. A two-seat all-metal aircraft with a low wing, the K47 was fitted with a Bristol Jupiter VII radial engine and flew in January 1929. It had a high performance for its day, being capable of a speed of 289 km/h (180 mph) at 3050 m (10,000 ft). Armament

WWI ace Ernst Udet was a national hero in Germany. When he was persuaded to join the new Nazi *Luftwaffe*, he was to play a major part in shaping the design of the new generation of warplanes with which it would be equipped.

comprised one rearward-firing and two forward-firing machine guns. It was produced in small numbers, most examples being delivered to China. The prototype K47 was allocated the Swedish registration S-AABW (later SE-ABW); it found its way to Germany in March 1934, after the Treaty of Versailles was repudiated by the new Nazi regime, whereupon it was given the German civil registration D-2012. A civil version of the K47, powered by a 540hp Siemens piston engine, was designated Junkers A48 and used as a mail carrier. Like the K47, the A48 was produced in small numbers and exported.

Before this, Hugo Junkers had founded his factory at Dessau, and had produced a series of all-metal commercial aircraft beginning with the single-engined Junkers F.13, which could be used as a landplane or a floatplane and which made a huge impact on the commercial aviation market worldwide. It was followed by the W.33, which in 1928 made the first east-west crossing of the Atlantic by a heavier-than-air machine (the British airship R.34 having first made the crossing in 1919), and by a succession of multi-engined types culminating in the Junkers Ju 52 of 1932, which in its tri-motor

form as the Ju 52/3m was the most prolific airliner in the world during the 1930s.

In 1933, after much clandestine preparation, the creation of Germany's new *Luftwaffe* got under way, and – thanks to the retention of a hard core of experienced aviation officers within the *Reichswehr* – the lessons of the 1914-18 air war had not been forgotten. One of those lessons was the importance of saturating the battle area with air power, a doctrine that involved not only attacks on enemy columns and troop concentrations, but also precision attacks on choke points such as bridges. In this respect the key word was 'precision', and the dive bomber was the ideal vehicle for this type of attack. At least, there was no doubt about this in the mind of one man in particular.

Father of the Stuka

Ernst Udet was Germany's second-ranking air ace of World War I, with 62 victories to his credit. After the war, Udet had established a reputation as a skilled and daredevil pilot, taking part in films and exhibitions in Europe and the United States. In September 1931, Udet was in the USA to participate in the National Air Races at Cleveland, Ohio, when he had the chance to inspect the Curtiss F8C Helldiver, a biplane then being developed as a dive-bomber for the US Navy. Udet witnessed the aircraft make a high-speed diving 'attack' on the airfield at the climax of its display, and was impressed. So, when they saw the film of this event, were the Junkers designers and engineers at Dessau. This sudden upsurge of interest in the dive-bomber concept led to dive bombing trials being carried out in Sweden with the K47, using practice bombs provided by Bofors.

In 1933, Ernst Udet contacted a senior official in the *Reichsluftministerium*, Franz Müller, and recommended the purchase of two Curtiss XF11C biplanes for evaluation. The suggestion reached the ears of Hermann Goering, the Nazi government's newly-appointed air minister, who had flown alongside Udet in World War I. Goering, who had made several unsuccessful attempts to persuade Udet to become involved with the clandestine *Luftwaffe*, now seized the opportunity to bring his former brother officer into the Nazi circle. He gave his personal

Hugo Junkers ensured his firm's postwar success with a series of very effective commercial aircraft designs like the G.24 all-metal commercial airliner, about 70 of which were built. (*Lufthansa*)

approval to the purchase, and authorized the transfer of funds to the German Embassy in Washington DC to cover the cost. Accompanied by Udet, who had been in the United States for some weeks testing new racing aeroplanes on behalf of Curtiss, the two aircraft were shipped to Bremerhaven aboard the liner *Europa* in October 1933 and were forwarded to the new experimental test centre at Rechlin, north of Berlin, where they were uncrated and assembled in readiness for the planned trials.

American inspiration

The two aircraft were Export Type II models of the Curtiss XF11C-2 Goshawk, the prototype of which had flown for the first time in March 1932. Powered by a 715-hp Wright Cyclone radial engine, the aircraft was a larger development of the F8C and was designed as a fighter-bomber; during the early 1930s it was to be widely exported, the biggest overseas customer being China, which also built the type under licence. The aircraft acquired by Germany were given the registrations D-IRIS and D-ISIS. On 20 July, 1935, Ernst Udet was demonstrating D-IRIS over Berlin's Tempelhof airport when the tail came off in a dive; Udet parachuted to safety, but the aircraft was a total

loss. The other aircraft, having completed its evaluation, was used by Udet as his personal aircraft. Udet was now a firm member of the Nazi establishment, having been appointed Director of Fighters and Dive Bombers in the *Luftwaffe*. He retained the use of D-ISIS until the outbreak of World War II, when he presented the aircraft to the Berlin Air Museum. After many of the museum's prized exhibits were destroyed in a RAF bombing raid, the survivors, including D-ISIS, were removed to a safer location in Poland. After the war, D-ISIS was seized by the Polish authorities and placed on display at the Polish National Air Museum, at Krakow.

The Goshawk and the K47 were not the only types to undergo dive-bombing trials at Rechlin. Another was the Heinkel He 50 reconnaissance bomber, which first flew in 1932 and which was produced in small numbers. Interestingly enough, the He 50 was to make its mark as a dive bomber in a roundabout way. The type was designated He 66 for export, and several were delivered to Japan in 1933. There, the He 66 was modified by the Aichi company and developed into the D1A1, the first of a series of dive bombers culminating in the D3A 'Val', which was to cause such devastation at

The four-engined Junkers G.38 was the largest commercial aircraft of its time. Note the patent Junkers double-wing ailerons and hydraulically-operated flaps, which were also a feature of the Stuka. (*Lufthansa*)

Pearl Harbor in December 1941. Two He 50s were used in the Rechlin dive-bombing trials, both being powered by Pratt & Whitney Hornet radial engines.

In January 1935, the *Reichsluftministerium* launched an industrial competition for the development of an aircraft in the category of *Sturzkampfflugzeug* (dive bomber), even though its senior officials were by no means unanimously in favour of the concept. *Major* Wolfram Freiherr von Richthofen, heading the Development Section of the Air Ministry's technical department, thought that such an aircraft would be far too vulnerable to ground fire, while *Oberst* Erhard Milch, the Secretary of State for Air, believed that crews would not be able to withstand the high gravitational forces to which they would be subjected during dive-bombing operations.

Competing designs

Four German firms entered designs. One of them was a new concern; in July 1933, the Blohm und Voss shipbuilding company in Hamburg had formed an aviation subsidiary,

the Hamburger Flugzeugbau GmbH, whose contender was the Ha 137. From the longer-established Arado Flugzeugwerke GmbH came the Arado Ar 81, while Ernst Heinkel AG, which had just opened a new factory at Rostock, entered the He 118. The Junkers entry was designed by Dipl-Ing Hermann Pohlmann, a former aviator who had been shot down and taken prisoner by the British in 1917; he had been part of the Junkers concern since 1923. A wooden mock-up of his design had been built at Dessau in 1934, and work now proceeded on a flying prototype, designated Ju 87V-1. The aircraft was powered by a 525-hp Rolls-Royce Kestrel 12-cylinder, liquid-cooled engine and featured twin fins and rudders. Early trials showed that the engine was prone to overheating, a problem caused not by the powerplant but by the radiator, which was too small. It was easily cured by fitting a radiator of larger dimensions.

The first of three Arado Ar 81 prototypes, the Ar 81V-1, flew in 1935 and carried the civil registration D-UJOX. Both the Ar 81V-1 and V-2 (D-UPAR) had slim, boom-like rear fuselages

Junkers' most famous commercial design was the Ju 52/3m, which was the subject of worldwide commercial sales and which also was widely used by the military. (*Lufthansa*)

and oval end-plate twin fin and rudder assemblies, but the third aircraft, Ar 81V-3 D-UDEX, which was flown and tested in 1936, had a single fin and rudder and a deeper rear fuselage than its two predecessors. The Ar 81 was of all-metal construction and was the only one of the four contenders to retain a biplane configuration, a fact that played a considerable part in its rejection.

Better than Junkers?

The Hamburger Flugzeugbau's design team began work on a single-seat dive bomber late in 1933, the first project being designated P.6. This was to have had a BMW 15 engine, but as this powerplant was not yet available, the design was modified to take the Pratt and Whitney Hornet (which was later licence-built as the BMW 132) and redesignated P.6a. The project designation was eventually changed to Ha 137, and work was begun on two prototypes powered by the Hornet, the Ha 137V-1 (D-IXAX) and Ha 137V-2 (D-IBGI), together with one prototype powered by the Rolls-Royce Kestrel V, the Ha 137V-3 (D-IZIQ), or P.6b. All

three prototypes were completed during 1934-35, and after initial flight tests at Hamburg dive-bombing trials were undertaken at Travemünde. By this time it had become obvious that the somewhat large Hornet radial engine was unsuited to the single-seat dive bomber configuration because it severely restricted the pilot's view forward, and when the new Junkers Jumo 210 liquid-cooled in-line engine became available in 1936, two more prototypes were built around this powerplant.

Powered by the 610-hp Jumo 210Aa, the new aircraft were the Ha 137V-4 (D-IFOE) and V-5 (D-IUXU). The radial-engined and in-line engined versions were respectively designated Ha 137A and Ha 137B, the latter being the proposed production version. The Ha 137 was designed around a wing based on a single strong tubular spar which also served as the fuel tank. It was tough and manoeuvrable, and a certain amount of surprise was expressed in some quarters when it lost out to the Ju 87. The decision, however, had political undertones, as the Blohm und Voss concern was originally of Jewish origin.

In many respects, the Blohm & Voss Ha 137 was a better aircraft than the Ju 87. However, political (and racial) considerations rather than technical capability played a major part in its demise. (*via Phil Jarrett*)

As a matter of interest, the Hornet-engined Ha 137 was also intended for use by the German Navy, and two navalised versions were projected, the P.11a with wheels and the P.11b with floats. As an insurance against the failure of the Ha 137, the Hamburger Flugzeugbau design team also produced an alternative dive bomber design, the Cyclone-powered P.7 biplane, which was not built.

Aesthetically the most attractive of the entrants in the Stuka design competition, the Heinkel He 118 was nevertheless inferior in performance to the Ju 87. Four prototypes were built, the first and second aircraft both being fitted with the Rolls-Royce Kestrel engine. The He 118V-1 was lost when it broke up in mid-air while being piloted by Ernst Udet. The cause of the accident was attributed to excessive engine vibration, brought about by the pilot's unfamiliarity with the automatic propeller pitch change mechanism. The He 118V-3 was fitted with the DB 600 engine, while the V-4 had the DB 601. The He 118V-3 and V-4 were subsequently exported to Japan, one for evaluation by the Japanese Navy and the other by the Army. The He 118V-2 was used by the Heinkel factory as a turbojet test-bed, being used to flight test the Heinkel-Hirth HeS 3B

before this engine was installed in the Heinkel He 178, the world's first jet aircraft.

Light attackers

Hugo Junkers never lived to witness the maiden flight of the Ju 87V-1, which occurred on 17 September 1935; he had died in the previous February. Meanwhile, the dive bomber requirement had devolved into two separate classes, one calling for a light single-seat aircraft and the other for a heavier two-seat machine. The prototypes of the two contenders in the first class, the Henschel Hs 123V-1 and the Fieseler Fi 98a, both made their appearance in the spring of 1935. The Henschel made its public debut on 8 May, when it was flown by Ernst Udet at the Henschel Flugzeugwerke factory airfield at Johannisthal, near Berlin. It was soon apparent that the Hs 123 was greatly superior to the Fi 98a, which was abandoned.

The prototype Henschel Hs 123V-1 flew for the first time in May 1935 and the type was ordered into production, five Hs 123As being sent to Spain for operational evaluation with the Condor Legion in 1936. This resulted in the improved Hs 123B, which saw combat during the German invasions of Poland, France and the USSR. Some Hs 123s were still operational

The Heinkel He 118 was undoubtedly the best- and cleanest-looking of the Stuka competitors, although it was not a great performer. The prototype broke up in mid-air, probably because of test pilot Ernst Udet's inability to manage the propeller pitch mechanism properly. (via Phil Jarrett)

on the Eastern Front until 1944, when the type was finally withdrawn. The Hs 123C was a variant armed with 20-mm cannon.

On 1 October, 1935, the *Luftwaffe* had set up an experimental dive bomber *gruppe* at Schwerin; this was subsequently designated I/*Stukageschwader* 162 (I/StG 162), the first *Gruppe* of the famous 'Immelmann' *Geschwader*. The unit was named after the first German air ace of World War I, Max Immelmann, a leading pioneer of air fighting tactics. This *Gruppe*, together with two more, II/StG 162 and I/StG 165, was originally equipped with He 50s, He 51s and Ar 65s, but in the autumn of 1936 it received its first Henschel Hs 123A-1s.

Heavy Stukas

Meanwhile, the choice of aircraft to meet the requirement for the heavy two-seat Stuka had been narrowed down to the Ju 87 and the He 118. It seemed that the latter might have a fighting chance of being awarded the potentially lucrative contract when, on 24 January 1936, the Ju 87V-1 prototype entered an uncontrollable inverted spin at Dessau and crashed, fatally injuring its two crew members. Then, on 27 July, 1936, Ernst Udet took off in the Heinkel He 118V-1, which bore the civil

registration D-UKYM, to carry out some high-speed dives over Lake Müritz. As Udet was on the point of pulling out, the engine tore away from its mountings and the aircraft literally broke up around him. His seat belt broke and he struggled clear of the wreckage, opening his parachute a couple of thousand feet above the ground. He received slight injuries on landing.

As a result of the accident to the Ju 87V-1, the second prototype, the Ju 87V-2, was fitted with a single fin and rudder. It was also given a new engine, the 610-hp Junkers Jumo 210a. Registered D-UHUH, it had joined the trials programme at Rechlin in March 1936, and following the crash of the Heinkel 118 it was declared the winner of the contest.

While the contending aircraft were being evaluated, intensive trials were also conducted with bombs of various weight and with the *Stuvi* bombsight, this being an abbreviation of *Stukavisier*. The sight was progressively refined as the trials progressed, test flights being undertaken by Heinkel He 50s and a Junkers A48. In March 1936 an He 50 was flying with a *Stuvi* A2 bombsight, together with an ETC 500 bomb rack, capable of carrying a 500-kg (1102-lb) bomb.

Before being delivered to Rechlin, the

The Ju 87V-1 prototype being refuelled at Dessau during the autumn of 1935. The dive brakes have not yet been fitted, although their mountings are visible. (*via Phil Jarrett*)

Another view of the Ju 87V-1, which had a 640-hp Rolls-Royce Kestrel engine. The prototype was destroyed on 24 January 1936, when it entered an inverted spin and crashed at Dessau, killing its crew. (*via Phil Jarrett*)

The second prototype Junkers Ju 87V-2, D-UHUH, was powered by a 610-hp Junkers Jumo 210A engine. It featured a single fin and rudder, a modification incorporated after the loss of the Ju 87V-1. *(via Phil Jarrett)*

Ju 87V-2 had been fitted with special slats beneath the wing, just outboard of the undercarriage fairings. These could be rotated downwards through 90 degrees to act as dive brakes. The single 500-kg (1102-lb) bomb was carried on a special under-fuselage cradle hinged just aft of the radiator bath; this was swung forward during the dive, enabling the weapon to clear the propeller arc when released.

The Ju 87V-3, D-UKYQ, was similar to the modified V-2, but had an improved forward view. The fourth aircraft, Ju 87V-4 D-UBIP, was the production prototype; it made its first flight in the autumn of 1936 and was delivered to Rechlin early in November. There it began a series of intensive dive-bombing trials, lasting six months. In addition to carrying out tests with 250-kg (551-lb) and 500-kg (1102-lb) bombs, the aircraft also dropped SC 10 anti-personnel fragmentation bombs, which proved extremely effective against 'soft' targets such as parked aircraft.

Ten pre-production Ju 87A-0 aircraft, produced in the last six months of 1936, were followed by the production Ju 87A-1, the first examples of which were delivered to I/StG 162 'Immelmann' in the spring of 1937. The Ju 87A-1, nicknamed the *Anton* (the German phonetic alphabet word for the letter 'A') retained the large 'trouser' undercarriage legs of the prototypes and the Ju 87A-0, but had straight wing leading edges instead of the double-tapered section that characterized earlier machines.

Tested in combat

In December 1937, three Ju 87A-1 aircraft were sent to Spain to be evaluated under combat conditions with the Condor Legion, the air component of which was commanded by *Generalleutnant* Wolfram von Richthofen. Hitherto, von Richthofen had been a strong critic of the dive-bomber concept, but after seeing the three Stukas perform in Spain he became a convert. Pilots of StG 162 were sent to Spain in relays to fly the Ju 87A-1 operationally, developing basic dive-bombing tactics, air-to-ground communications techniques and target location procedures. The Stukas always operated under strong fighter escort, so that Republican aircraft were safely kept at arm's length.

By the end of November 1937, 27 Ju 87A-1s had been delivered to the *Luftwaffe*. This model was followed by the generally similar A-2, which had improved radio equipment. About 200 examples of the A series were built before production switched to the greatly improved Ju 87B, or *Bertha*, which incorporated many features inspired by lessons learned in Spain.

Early in 1938, a standard Ju 87A-1 was taken from the production line at Dessau and, fitted with a 1000-hp Junkers Jumo 211A engine,

The Ju 87V-3, D-UKYQ, was similar to the V-2, but had a modified tailplane with square tips and a full-span elevator. The aircraft's huge flap area is shown to good advantage in this photograph. (*via Phil Jarrett*)

became the Ju 87B *Bertha*. The Ju 87B had an enlarged vertical tail, redesigned crew canopy and new cantilever fairings over the main undercarriage legs, with 'spats' instead of 'trousers'. The Ju 87B was to be the main production version of the Stuka.

Stuka construction

The Ju 87's fuselage was built in two oval sections, joined along the centreline at the side. Construction comprised a semi-monocoque of frames and stringers, the frame being of Z-section riveted to the all-metal stressed skin. The fuselage was flush-riveted on all external surfaces. The U-section stringers were joined to the skin by a double line of rivets, continuous throughout the frames. A curved angle bracket was riveted to both frame and stringer at each frame junction. In the lower fuselage the stringers were fitted very closely together, and very strong frames were fitted where the spars passed through. The addition of thick plating meant that the fuselage was very strong, and well able to withstand the forces experienced in a dive and the subsequent pull-out. The two crew positions were separated by an anti-crash

hoop made of cast magnesium, designed to prevent crushing of the cockpit area should the aircraft turn over on its back as the result of a ground accident.

Wings

The low-mounted cantilever wing was built in three sections. The centre section, which carried the undercarriage attachments, was an integral part of the fuselage, the port and starboard outer sections being secured to the centre section by ball-and-socket joints on the spar flanges. The centre section was set at an anhedral angle of 12 degrees from the fuselage sides, while the outer sections had a dihedral of 8 degrees, producing the famous 'inverted gull wing' arrangement that was the Stuka's main recognition feature. This configuration had a number of advantages, not least of which was the reduction in the height of the undercarriage, thereby saving weight. It also offered improved crew vision and had the effect of reducing drag between the wing and fuselage.

The wings were constructed around two spars with extruded L-section flanges riveted together through flat plate webs. Smooth

D-IEAU was an early production Ju 87A-1. The number '12' on the rear fuselage, near the bracing strut, possibly indicates that this was the twelfth aircraft to emerge from the production line at Dessau. (*via Phil Jarrett*)

stressed metal skinning was flush-riveted to closely-spaced rib sections extending across the chord. The wing was fitted with Junkers double-wing ailerons and hydraulically operated flaps divided into three sections extending along the mainplane trailing edge, an arrangement first used on the Ju 52 transport and patented by the firm. Hydraulically-actuated dive brakes rotating downwards through 90 degrees were fitted under the leading edge of each wing, attached to the front spar outboard of the undercarriage legs.

Tail Unit

The tail unit of the Ju 87 (with the exception of the Ju 87V-1) comprised a single cantilever fin and rudder, the tailplane being braced with V-struts to two points on the lower fuselage. The tailplane was rectangular, the fin and rudder square-cut. The whole fin area was covered by flush-riveted metal skin. Automatic tail trimming by mechanical linkage to the flaps was used to maintain trim during flap selection. Elevators and rudder were both fitted with trim tabs, which could be adjusted in flight. An auxiliary control surface on the starboard elevator, which was automatically under tension when the dive brakes were extended, disengaged when the bomb release mechanism was activated and served as an automatic pull-out device.

Cockpit

The Ju 87 carried a crew of two, comprising pilot and gunner, seated back to back in tandem under a fully transparent canopy. From the Ju 87B onwards, the gunner was also responsible for operating the radio equipment, leaving the pilot completely free to control the aircraft and operate its offensive weapons. In an emergency, the whole canopy could be jettisoned in one piece by pulling a lever.

Powerplant

All production Ju 87s with the exception of the Ju 87A series, which had the Junkers Jumo 210, were fitted with various marks of the 12-cylinder, inverted-Vee, liquid-cooled Jumo 211. The engine was slung between two cantilever magnesium castings, being secured to the airframe by four Junkers ball-and-socket joints, and could be easily removed with the use of simple block and tackle gear, which greatly facilitated maintenance at forward airstrips. Removal of the whole engine took about 20 minutes. The aircraft was fitted with a three-blade, two-position Jumo-Hamilton HPA III propeller with automatic rpm governor.

Armament

The Ju 87A was limited to the carriage of a single 500-kg (1102-lb) bomb on the under-

A Ju 87A-1 wearing the standard 'semi-splinter' camouflage adopted by the *Luftwaffe* prior to World War II. The white circle on which the Swastika was previously superimposed is no longer in use. (*via Phil Jarrett*)

An early production Ju 87B seen in early *Luftwaffe* markings, with full red, white and black tail insignia. The aircraft's dive brakes, fully extended, are clearly visible in this photograph. (*via Phil Jarrett*)

Junkers Ju 87B aircraft on the assembly line at the Dessau factory. Early production of the Stuka was divided between Dessau and the Weser plant at Tempelhof Airport, Berlin. (*via Phil Jarrett*)

fuselage bomb cradle, but on the Ju 87B the carrier was strengthened to carry up to 1000 kg (2204 lb), and EC 50 racks for the carriage of smaller bombs were fitted under the outer wings. Ultimately, the Stuka would be able to carry up to 1800 kg (3986 lb) of bombs under the fuselage, as well as various stores on underwing hardpoints.

Ju 87Bs in Spain

In October 1938, six months before the end of the savage civil war in Spain, five early production Ju 87Bs joined the Condor Legion for operational evaluation, and confirmed the success of the earlier Ju 87A. Meanwhile, the Ju 87B order book was increasing steadily. By 1 March, 1939, 964 Ju 87Bs were on order, of which 187 had either been delivered or were awaiting delivery. By the end of July, the number of Ju 87B-1s delivered had risen to 435,

enabling the A-series aircraft to be withdrawn and re-assigned to various training establishments. Production was now divided between Dessau and Weser/Tempelhof, but a major new factory was in the process of being established at Bremen-Lemwerder, and this would be responsible for mass-producing the lion's share of Ju 87Bs.

The total number of Ju 87B-1s on order in August 1939 was 803, with a follow-on order for 827 B-2s, the latter fitted with a 1200-hp Jumo 211Da engine with direct fuel injection. The B-2, which was scheduled to make its appearance in December 1939, had hydraulically-operated radiator cooling gills and modified undercarriage legs, and could carry a 1000 kg (2204 lb) bomb load.

Also on order were 170 examples of the Ju 87C, a special conversion of the dive bomber intended for operation from the aircraft carrier

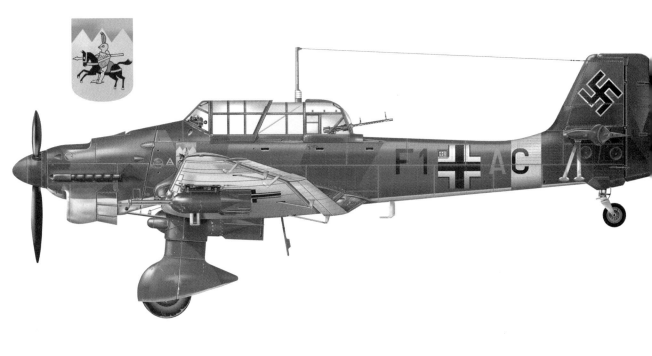

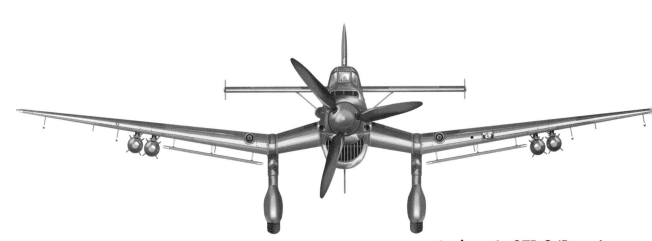

Junkers Ju 87B-2 'Berta'
Major Helmut Bode
Commander III/StG 77
Eastern Front (Sevastopol)
June 1942

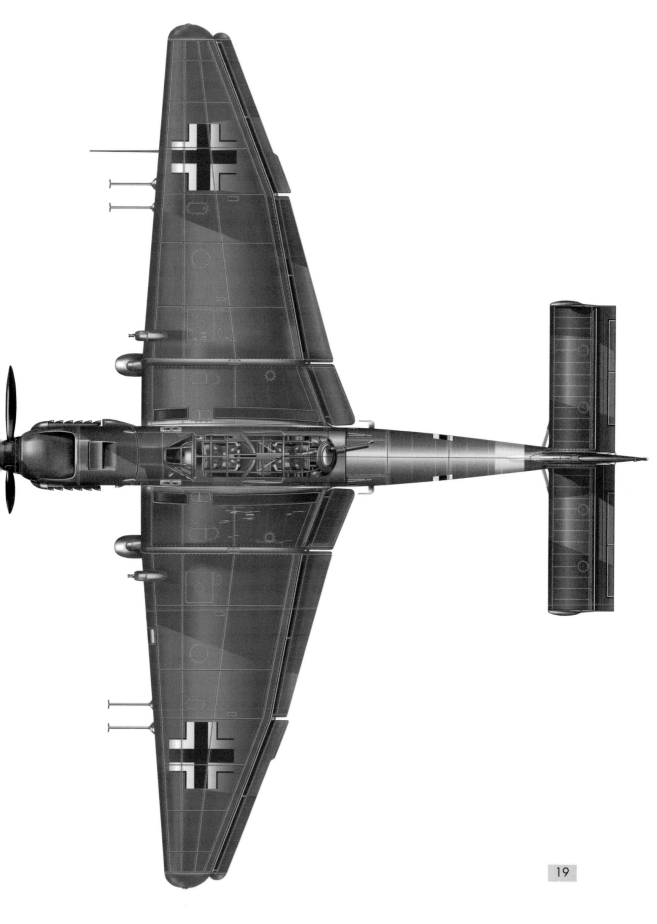

Five Ju 87Bs were sent to Spain in October 1938 to be evaluated under combat conditions, and proved even more successful than the trio of Ju 87As that had preceded them. (*via Phil Jarrett*)

Graf Zeppelin, which was under construction at Kiel. The *staffel* that was to operate these aircraft, 4.(Stuka) 186, had already been formed in December 1938, and since then had been training at Kiel-Holtenau, first with Ju 87As and then with *Berthas*, which it had received in May 1939.

Ready for war

In August 1939, nine Stuka *gruppen* totalling 219 aircraft stood ready to take part in the planned assault on Poland. One of these units, I/StG 76, suffered a catastrophic accident on 15 August, shortly after it had moved to Cottbus, Silesia, from its usual base at Graz, in Austria. On that day, the *gruppe* was detailed to carry out a dive-bombing demonstration over the Neuhammer range for the benefit of some senior staff officers. Weather conditions dictated that the dive would have to be made through cloud, but the weather report indicated that there would be plenty of clearance between the cloud base and the ground. Unfortunately the report was wrong, and while still in cloud 13 Stukas dived headlong into a forest, killing all 26 crew members. The exact circumstances behind the accident were never established, although faulty altimeter settings were held to be the primary cause.

Engineers bringing together the component parts of a Ju 87B. By the last day of August 1939, 437 Ju 87Bs had been delivered to the *Luftwaffe*. (*via Phil Jarrett*)

2. Operational History 1939-40: Blitzkrieg and Battle of Britain

At 04.45 on 1 September, 1939, three Junkers Ju 87B Stukas of III/ *Stukageschwader* 1, flying from Elbing, made a low-level attack on the steel bridges spanning the river Vistula at Dirschau. The bridges were to have been seized by the German 7th Airborne Division, but the planned airdrop was frustrated by fog. The Stukas' task was to destroy the strongpoints from which demolition charges would be fired by Polish engineers. The three aircraft dropped three 250-kg (551-lb) and a dozen 50-kg (110-lb) bombs on their targets. The attack was led by *Oberleutnant* Bruno Dilley. The *Luftwaffe*'s first mission of the war was only a partial success, as one of the bridges was blown soon afterwards. An hour later, the strongpoints were attacked again by a flight of Dornier Do 17Z bombers of III/KG 3 from Heilingenbeil.

As the morning fog cleared, 36 Henschel Hs 123 assault aircraft of II/LG 2 bombed and strafed Polish positions in the village of Pryzstain. This was the first instance in World War II in which the *Luftwaffe* carried out direct support operations in conjunction with ground forces. At about the same time, 60 Heinkel 111s of I and III/KG 4 dropped 48 tons of bombs on airfields in the Krakow area; later, further attacks on these airfields were made by Dornier 17s and Ju 87s of StG 1.

In the course of another attack, Stukas of StG 2 encountered PZL P.11C fighters of the Polish Air Force's 111/2 *Dyon* (Squadron) which had taken off to intercept a formation of Heinkels. One P.11C was shot down by a Stuka.

In the afternoon, a Polish cavalry brigade, advancing towards the German frontier from Wielun, was heavily attacked by Stukas of StG 2 and I/StG 77, followed by Dornier Do 17s of KG 77. The destruction of the brigade was complete after 90 individual aircraft sorties had been flown against it.

On 2 September, continued attacks by Stukas inflicted further heavy losses on Polish ground forces. Airfields in the Deblin area were attacked by 88 Heinkel He 111s of KG 4 and Messerschmitt Bf 110s of ZG 76. Following the airfield attacks, Stuka and other units struck at lines of communication, supply and ammunition dumps and also bombed harbour installations, warships and coastal batteries.

The Stuka unit originally formed for service on the aircraft carrier *Graf Zeppelin* , IV/StG 186, was heavily involved in these actions, as were two *Gruppen* of StG 2 and IV/LG 1. The latter unit, commanded by *Hauptmann* Koegl, was beginning to specialize in anti-shipping operations; on the previous day it had sunk the Polish torpedo boat *Mazur* in Oksywie harbour, and now, on 2 September, its bombs sent the auxiliary vessels *Gdansk* and *Gdynie* to the bottom in the Gulf of Danzig. On 3 September IV/StG 186 was again in action against Polish shipping, sinking the destroyer *Wicher* and the minelayer *Gryf*.

On 9 September, with the German armies about to complete a pincer movement around the Polish capital, Warsaw, the Poles launched a desperate counter-attack on the river Bzura, aimed at the exposed flank of the German 8th

Stukas in echelon formation, en route to Poland in September 1939. The Stukas suffered a catastrophe just prior to the Polish campaign, when 13 aircraft of StG 76 dived into the ground in fog during a demonstration formation attack. (via Phil Jarrett)

Army. As the threat developed, General von Rundstedt, commanding Army Group South, called for a maximum air effort. Between 9 and 12 September, massed dive-bomber attacks were launched from forward airstrips. The impetus of the Polish attack was halted by the destruction of the bridges over the Bzura, and then the main elements of the Polish force were broken up by two days of air attacks by Stukas, Heinkels, Dorniers and Hs 123s. The 200,000 troops of the Army of Poznan were isolated, surrounded and subjected to almost continual air attack until their surrender on 19 September.

On 13 September, the *Luftwaffe* carried out the first phase of *Unternehmen Seebad* (Operation *Seaside*), the massed air attack on Warsaw. A total of 183 bombers and Stukas attacked the north-west district of the city, causing severe damage. Four days later, in accordance with a secret German-Soviet agreement on the partition of Poland, Soviet forces invaded the country from the east. The next day, the remnants of the Polish Air Force were evacuated to neutral Romania.

On 25 September, following the dropping of propaganda leaflets on Warsaw urging the garrison to surrender, 400 bombers – including eight *Stukagruppen* – attacked the city in relays beginning at 0800. Thirty Junkers Ju 52 transports were also employed as makeshift bombers, their crews shovelling incendiary bombs through open loading doors. By the end of the day, 500 tons of high explosive and 72 tons of incendiaries had been dropped on Warsaw, whose garrison surrendered on 27 September. On the same day the garrison at Modlin also capitulated, the town having been subjected to severe air raids for 36 hours. The

A Ju 87B-1 about to start its dive. This photograph was taken early in 1940, and the aircraft is not carrying external armament. (*via Phil Jarrett*)

last organized Polish resistance to the invaders ended on 5 October.

The Stukas had escaped comparatively lightly during the Polish campaign, 31 having been lost out of a total of 285 German aircraft destroyed. The campaign had amply vindicated the concept of the Stuka as a close support and precision attack aircraft, but it was apparent that its success in the 'flying artillery' role had been largely due to the absence of determined fighter opposition. The Polish fighter pilots had fought with great gallantry, and when they did succeed in engaging enemy bombers they inflicted substantial losses, but with most of their air assets destroyed on the ground there was little they could do to stave off the inevitable end.

However, the Polish campaign revealed a number of shortcomings in the Ju 87B Stuka. The aircraft lacked adequate defensive armament, it needed more armour protection for the crew, and it would have to be fitted with a more powerful engine if larger bombs were to be carried. Modifying the Ju 87B to fulfil these criteria would take time, and the modified aircraft would not be ready in time for the campaigns that were being planned for the spring of 1940. But there was another problem that could more easily be rectified. It was one of range.

Norway 1940

The long-range version of the basic Ju 87B was the Ju 87R, the new suffix denoting *Reichweite* (range). The airframe was modified to take an extra 150-l (33 Imp gal) tank in each wing, and was fitted with underwing points for two 300-l (66 Imp gal) drop tanks. The Ju 87R-1 had a range of 1410 km (876 miles) as compared with the 550 km (342 miles) of the Ju 87B-1. Known as the *Richard*, the Ju 87R was not operational in time for the invasion of Norway, which began on 9 April 1940, but began to reach the operational Stuka units early in May.

Only one *Stukageschwader*, StG 1, was assigned to the Norwegian campaign. This operation, code-named *Weserübung* (Exercise *Weser*) got off to a bad start when the German heavy cruiser *Blücher* was heavily damaged by the guns of Feste Oskarsborg, the powerful fortress commanding the approaches to Oslo,

and then sunk by torpedoes with the loss of 1000 lives. Oskarsborg and the neighbouring fortress of Akershus were attacked by 22 Stukas of I/StG 1, led by *Hauptmann* Paul-Werner Hozzel, and the main armaments of the strongpoints were put out of action. In the afternoon, I/StG 1's Stukas deployed from their base at Kiel-Holtanau to Oslo's Fornebu airport, newly captured by German airborne forces. A forward operating base was established at Stavanger-Sola, which had also been captured earlier on 9 April.

Lack of range prevented the Stukas from mounting attacks on British warships in the Norwegian Sea, but some effective bombing was carried out by horizontal bombers. Towards noon on 9 April, units of the British Fleet off Bergen were attacked by 41 Heinkel He 111s of KG 26 and 47 Junkers Ju 88s of KG 30. The battleship HMS *Rodney* was hit by a bomb which failed to explode, the cruisers HMS *Devonshire*, HMS *Southampton* and HMS *Glasgow* were all damaged, and the destroyer HMS *Gurkha* was sunk west of Stavanger.

British dive bombers strike

On 10 April, there was a demonstration of how effective the dive bomber could be in a precision attack on shipping – but it was the British who provided it. Early that morning, 16 Blackburn Skua dive bombers of the Fleet Air Arm – seven from No 800 Squadron and nine from No 103 – took off from Hatston, north of Kirkwall in the Orkneys. Each aircraft carried a 227-kg (500-lb) bomb. Their target was a German naval force at Bergen, which included the light cruisers *Koenigsberg* and *Köln* and the gunnery training ship *Bremse*.

After a 482 km (300 mile) flight, the Skuas – their number reduced to 15 after one aircraft returned with engine trouble – attacked the *Koenigsberg* in line astern, diving from 2440 m (8000 ft). The bombing was highly accurate and the cruiser, having suffered three direct hits and a dozen near misses, exploded and sank. She was the first major warship to be sunk solely by air attack in combat. One Skua was shot down by AA fire.

The Blackburn Skua two-seat naval dive bomber was in many ways the British equivalent of the Stuka. It was designed to meet

French marines of the Allied Expeditionary Force examine a Blackburn Skua dive-bomber in northern Norway, May 1940. The operations around Narvik were beyond the range of even the Ju 87R, until the Germans could capture an airfield closer to the battle area. (*ECP Armées*)

the requirements of Specification O.27/34, and the prototype was flown in 1937. The Skua was the first monoplane to be adopted by the Royal Navy, and, such was the pressing need for fleet protection against air attack, it saw more action as a fighter than it did in its intended role. In fact, the first German aircraft to fall victim to British fighters in World War 2, a Dornier Do 18 flying boat, was shot down in the North Sea by Skuas on 26 September 1939. Skuas operated in the North Sea, Atlantic and Mediterranean theatres, being replaced by Fairey Fulmars and Hawker Sea Hurricanes in 1941.

The middle of April 1940 found the Stukas of StG 1 operating from Vaernes airfield in central Norway, supporting German forces attacking the harbour town of Trondheim. Stukas fitted with skis also operated from a frozen lake at Jonsvannet. On 30 April, while the evacuation of Allied forces from Namsos was under way,

Stukas of I/StG 1 sank the anti-aircraft sloop HMS *Bittern*, which their crews mistook for a British cruiser, and on 3 May they sank the British destroyer HMS *Afridi* and the French destroyer *Bison*. A few days later, the first long-range Ju 87Rs began to reach StG 1, enabling the Stukas to operate as far north as Narvik, where an Allied expeditionary force had landed. Here, for the first time, the Stukas encountered Allied fighters in the shape of the Gloster Gladiators of No 236 Squadron, which were operating from rough landing grounds at Bardufoss and Bødo. On 27 May, the latter airstrip was heavily bombed and strafed by StG 1's Stukas and also by Messerschmitt Bf 110s of ZG 76, which had been detailed to escort the dive bombers. Two Gladiator pilots, Flight Lieutenant Caesar Hull and Lieutenant Antony Lydekker (a Fleet Air Arm pilot attached to the RAF), took off to intercept and both were

A Stuka pilot makes his exit from a Ju 87B of II/StG 2. Note the 'Mounted Knight' insignia on the engine cowling, the emblem of II/StG 2 (*Stab*), the staff or headquarters flight of the *Gruppe*. (*via Phil Jarrett*)

credited with a Junkers Ju 87 destroyed, but both British pilots were wounded and had to make forced landings.

On 28 May, the aircraft carrier HMS *Glorious* flew off 15 Hawker Hurricane fighters of No 46 Squadron, which joined the surviving Gladiators at Bardufoss. They were just in time to cover the final evacuation of Allied forces from Narvik and Halstad, both of which were heavily attacked by all available German aircraft in this closing phase of the campaign. The RAF fighters claimed nine German aircraft destroyed, including three Ju 87s, then flew away to land on the *Glorious*. The carrier was sunk on 8 June by the German battlecruisers *Scharnhorst* and *Gneisenau* while on her way to Scapa Flow, with the loss of all her aircraft and most of the aircrew.

The Battle of France

During the initial phase of the German attack on France and the Low Countries, which began on 10 May 1940 and involved air strikes on airfields and communications, *Luftwaffe* operations were the responsibility of *Fliegerkorps* I, II, IV and V, whose squadrons were equipped with Dornier 17s, Heinkel 111s and Junkers 88s. The *Stukageschwader* of *Fliegerkorps* VIII, commanded by *General-leutnant* Wolfram von Richthofen, were assigned to the direct support of General von Reichenau's Sixth Army and General Hoeppner's 6th *Panzerkorps*, whose task it would be to attack across the river Meuse. As a preliminary to this main offensive, some Stuka units were assigned to close support operations in the area of Liège, Belgium, the dive bombers being heavily escorted by the Messerschmitt Bf 109s of JG 27. The strong *Luftwaffe* participation in this sector was part of the overall German plan to convince the Allies that this was the focal point of the battlefront.

Then, on 13 May, the full weight of von Richthofen's *Stukageschwader* was thrown in to support the armoured thrust across the Meuse, the *Luftwaffe*'s orders being to pin down the French defences in the Sedan sector while the German ground forces established a bridgehead. This was achieved by relatively small formations of aircraft attacking in relays, rather than by a single all-out air attack.

A Ju 87B, coded TD+AY, releases a full weapons load in an attack against a coastal convoy over the English Channel. The *Luftwaffe* expected the Stuka to perform as well in the battle against the RAF as it had over France: they were in for a shock. (*via Phil Jarrett*)

The first phase opened on schedule at 1600 on 13 May, with a highly effective precision attack by Ju 87s of StG 77 on French artillery emplacements on the west bank of the Meuse. The total number of sorties flown by the *Luftwaffe* in the Sedan operation was about 700, including 200 by the Ju 87s of StG 2 and StG 77. Further north, the crossing of the Meuse at

Houx and Dinant was supported by the Stukas of StG 1 and the Dornier Do 17 medium bombers of KG 76 and KG 77.

On 15 May, with the Germans across the Meuse and the French defences at Sedan broken, the entire *Luftwaffe* effort was devoted to supporting the armoured dash to the Channel coast. This was where the Henschel Hs 126 observation aircraft came into their own; flying at low level and covered by Messerschmitt fighters, they continually reported the positions and movements of Allied units. It was in no small measure due to the activities of these spotter aircraft that the Panzer divisions were able to make such incredible headway in their race to the sea; flying ahead of the tanks, they would pick the likeliest routes and provide up-to-the-minute information on any opposition.

Combined arms

The deadly effectiveness of this spotter-Stuka-tank combination was demonstrated time and again during the campaign in France. One officer who experienced it was a certain Colonel Charles de Gaulle, whose 4th Armoured Division was badly mauled by Stukas during an attempted counter-attack at Montcornet on 18 May. It was a doubly bitter blow for de Gaulle, who had advocated just such a combination of spotter aircraft, close air support and armour just before the war – a recommendation which had been repeatedly ignored by the French High Command.

On 20 May, the 2nd Panzer Division reached the Somme estuary at Abbeville. It was less than a week since the French line had been broken at Sedan. The very speed with which they had achieved their objectives, however, placed the Germans in considerable danger. The tanks had advanced far ahead of their supporting infantry, and it would be some time before the newly-won ground could be consolidated; the situation was favourable for the Allies in the north to drive southwards and slice through the badly overstretched German armoured columns, trapping the Panzers against the coast and forging a strong link with Allied concentrations in the Amiens area.

On the morning of 22 May, German air reconnaissance reported a strong force of French armour and motorised infantry approaching Cambrai from the north. This was serious news, for all supplies for the German armoured group had to pass through the town, and as yet there were no combat forces to defend it. It was clear that the French armoured thrust would have to be checked before it presented a serious threat to Cambrai, and it was equally clear that only the *Luftwaffe* was in a position to do it.

The task was assigned to the Henschel 123s of II/LG 2 under the command of *Hauptmann* Otto Weiss, which shared Cambrai airfield with the Messerschmitt Bf 109s of its fighter escort *Gruppe*, I/JG 21. These two groups were the most advanced units of VIII *Fliegerkorps*. At 0900, four Hs 123s carried out an armed reconnaissance and confirmed that about 40 enemy tanks were only four miles from Cambrai. The armoured vehicles were in battle formation and travelling fast, and some distance to their rear a large dust cloud rose from a convoy of 150 trucks that carried French infantry. Led by Otto Weiss the four Henschels dived down to the attack, then raced for their base at low level. A few minutes later the rest of II/LG 2 took off, each aircraft armed with a pair of 45-kg (100-lb) bombs. The Henschels dived on the tanks in flights of three; their accuracy was phenomenal, and within a few minutes five of the French tanks were in flames and ten more had been halted, their tracks damaged by near-misses. At the same time, the Messerschmitts of I/JG 21 attacked the infantry convoy, sending the French troops scattering for cover. The attack was eventually stopped and turned back by accurate fire from the 88-mm guns of I/*Flakregiment* 33, two batteries of which were positioned on the approach to Cambrai.

British armoured threat

That same day, Stukas played a considerable part in containing an even more dangerous thrust by British armour and infantry in the Arras area, which came close to cutting General Erwin Rommel's 7th Panzer Division in two. The attack came as a salutary lesson to the future 'Desert Fox', who would never again leave his flanks unprotected.

By 23 May, the potential threat to the

Pilot and gunner climbing aboard a Ju 87B of *Lehrgeschwader* (LG) 1, whose 4.*Staffel* used the Ju 87 during the Battle of Britain. Getting into the Stuka appears to have required a certain amount of agility. (*via Phil Jarrett*)

advancing German armies had receded, and it was now clear that the Allied armies in Flanders were hopelessly trapped. The British Expeditionary Force, although still fighting hard around Lille and Arras, was falling back steadily towards the Channel ports, and the capture of these was the next step on the German timetable before launching a major offensive against the French armies in the south. By this time the leading elements of the German armour, curving up the coast from Abbeville, had reached Gravelines; the Panzers were, in fact, some 48 km (30 miles) nearer to the main evacuation port of Dunkirk than was the bulk of the BEF, and the stage seemed set for the German divisions to move in for the kill

here and at Calais and Boulogne.

From the air support standpoint, however, the tanks' headlong dash to the coast had created some serious problems. On 23 May the *Stukageschwader* of Richthofen's VIII *Fliegerkorps* were based at St Quentin after moving from one captured airstrip to another in the wake of the speeding armour, but even so the Channel ports were at the limit of the Ju 87B's combat radius, and the long-range Ju 87Rs were not yet deployed in significant numbers. If the Stukas were to be in a position to give maximum air support during the land assault on the ports it was obvious that the air units would have to be moved still further forward; but the ports were within easy reach of the RAF fighter bases in southern England, and von Richthofen was fully aware that if his dive bombers operated in this area without strong fighter escort they were likely to suffer severe losses. To ensure at least some protection for the Stukas during this preliminary phase of the battle for the ports, it was therefore decided to move one fighter *Gruppe* – I/JG 27 – to St Omer, which until a few hours earlier had been occupied by RAF units. On their approach to St Omer, however, the Messerschmitt pilots saw that a battle was still raging for possession of the airfield, and they were forced to divert to St Pol.

Battle for the Channel ports

The German air onslaught against Dunkirk was slow in developing. There were no major attacks on the port by VIII *Fliegerkorps* on 25 May, most of the aircraft being heavily committed elsewhere. StG 1 operated all day in support of German ground forces under heavy pressure from French armour which was counter-attacking in the Amiens sector, while StG 77 flew a series of counter-artillery operations near St Quentin and StG 2 furnished close support for the *Wehrmacht* units fighting in the streets of Boulogne and Calais. It was during these operations that StG 2 encountered Spitfires for the first time; the Messerschmitt escort managed to hold most of the British fighters at bay, but nevertheless four Stukas failed to return.

Boulogne fell on the morning of 25 May, and the *Stukageschwader* were now free to turn the full weight of their attacks on Calais, where the 10th Panzer Division was suffering badly from the gunfire of British and French warships lying offshore. At noon a call for assistance was received by VIII *Fliegerkorps*, and 40 Ju 87s took off to attack the vessels. For most of the pilots, it was their first mission against this type of target; as a result all of their bombs missed the warships, which were mostly destroyers and able to manoeuvre rapidly. As the Stukas formed up and headed for home they were attacked by Spitfires and three of the dive bombers were shot down.

At dawn the next day, at the request of General Heinz Guderian, commanding the German *Panzergruppe*, von Richthofen ordered every available Stuka unit to make an all-out attack on the town of Calais itself. The first attack was made by StG 77, escorted by all three *Gruppen* of JG 27, and it was followed up by StG 2. Wave after wave of Stukas pounded the Allied positions non-stop for an hour, this attack being followed up with an artillery barrage of fearsome intensity. At 1645 the Franco-British garrison of Calais – some 20,000 men, their supplies and ammunition exhausted – surrendered after fighting one of the most gallant defensive actions of the war.

The capture of Boulogne and Calais left Dunkirk as the only North Sea port still open for the evacuation of Allied troops. The German armoured spearheads were only 19 km (12 miles) from the port, and Admiral Sir Bertram Ramsay, directing the evacuation from Dover, counted on only two days of grace before Dunkirk fell into enemy hands. The British were as yet unaware that the Panzer divisions had come to a halt, and that the reduction of the Dunkirk pocket had been entrusted to the *Luftwaffe*. There was no sign of any major air offensive on 26 May; the port was attacked only by small formations of bombers from I and IV *Fliegerkorps*, operating from bases in Holland and the Rhine valley. The Stukas of VIII *Fliegerkorps* were still involved elsewhere, as was the only other *Luftwaffe* unit within reasonable striking distance of Dunkirk: I/KG 30, whose Junkers Ju 88s were based at Antwerp.

Bombing Dunkirk

The first real test came on 27 May, when successive formations of bombers drawn from *Fliegerkorps* I, II, IV and VIII began intensive attacks on the Dunkirk pocket and the armada of vessels assembled offshore. At first light, waves of Heinkel 111s of KG 1 and 4 bombed the port and the beaches, followed almost immediately by KG 54. The latter's bombs sank the 8000-ton French steamer *Aden* by the East Mole. At 0740 it was the turn of the Ju 87s of StG 2, which attacked the harbour and sank the troopship *Cote d'Azur*. Then came the Dornier 17s of KG 2 and 3, which set fire to the town's big oil storage tanks. A total of 300 German bombers attacked Dunkirk and its environs on 27 May during 12 raids, escorted by 550 fighter sorties. Their bombs turned the town into a

Ju 87Bs of 7./StG 1 preparing for a sortie from their airfield in the Pas de Calais during the Battle of Britain, in August 1940. Because of heavy losses, the Stuka was soon withdrawn from the battle. (*via Phil Jarrett*)

furnace; fires raged unchecked, as there had been no water supplies for five days, and by noon the air attacks had blocked the port. From then on, the evacuation had to be carried out via the beaches.

Regular patrols flown by the 16 Hurricane and Spitfire squadrons of No 11 Group, RAF Fighter Command, did little to mitigate the intensity of the attacks. In these early battles between the RAF and the *Luftwaffe*, both sides submitted claims in the heat of combat which were wildly exaggerated, but there was no escaping the fact that when the Stukas encountered RAF fighters, the dive-bombers suffered heavy casualties.

On 28 May the *Luftwaffe* made relatively few attacks on Dunkirk. The whole area was obscured by low cloud, mingling with the vast pall of smoke from the burning oil tanks. Conditions were generally unfavourable for the bombers, which instead were directed against the Belgian ports of Ostend and Nieuport. The low cloud persisted on 29 May, together with patches of fog and heavy rain.

During the night British engineers had managed to clear the harbour of Dunkirk sufficiently to allow the evacuation to resume, and throughout the morning of the 29th the long lines of weary troops filed aboard the waiting rescue vessels without interference from the *Luftwaffe*. Then, at about 1400, the clouds began to break up. Less than an hour later, all three *Stukageschwader* of VIII *Fliegerkorps* launched a savage attack on the harbour, hitting several vessels and rendering the quays unserviceable once more. Eleven of the 180 Junkers 87s involved in this raid were shot down, most of them by intense flak.

At 1530 the assault was taken up by the bombers of *Luftflotte* 2, including the Junkers Ju 88s of KG 30 from Antwerp and LG 1 from Düsseldorf. Their attacks were highly successful, with three British destroyers sunk and seven damaged. Five large steamers were also sunk during the day by Ju 87s and Ju 88s; the vessels were caught while in the process of embarkation and presented excellent stationary targets. The loss was keenly felt, and for several hours the evacuation was threatened with chaos; nevertheless, 47,310 troops were taken off the beaches that day.

The next morning – 30 May – found the beaches once again wrapped in rain and fog, and the *Luftwaffe* was powerless to intervene. Two *Stukagruppen* did take off, but they were unable to find targets and returned to base still carrying their bombs. On the last day of May bad weather again prevented the Germans from operating, apart from a few sorties by twin-engined bombers which resulted in the sinking of one large transport vessel.

All-out effort

Then came the morning of 1 June, and with it brilliant sunshine that brought the German aircraft down on the Dunkirk beaches in swarms. As well as the three *Stukageschwader*, the Ju 87s of I/StG 186 were also involved in the day's attacks, and were responsible for much of the Allied shipping losses, which included one French and three British destroyers, a minesweeper and two passenger ferries. I/StG 186 lost two Stukas to anti-aircraft fire, with another badly damaged by an RAF fighter; two aircraft were also lost by I/StG 77. The latter were possibly shot down by Lockheed Hudson aircraft of RAF Coastal Command, which reported several skirmishes with Stukas that day while flying the 'Sands Patrol', covering the evacuation forces.

The last major air attack on Dunkirk took place at 1100, when about 70 Dornier 17s, Heinkel 111s, Junkers 87s and Junkers 88s struck at fortifications and important bridges in the town. Fort Vallieres, one of the main strongpoints, was wiped out by dive bombers; the Stukas also damaged two vessels in the harbour. Subsequent attacks were carried out almost exclusively by the *Stukagruppen*; the twin-engined bombers were preparing for Operation *Paula*, a major attack on industrial targets in the Paris area which was scheduled for the next day. On 4 May the last Allied troops inside the Dunkirk perimeter – mostly French, who had held the line while over 366,000 men of the British Expeditionary Force and many of their own countrymen were evacuated – surrendered.

Battle for France

After a brief respite, the *Stukageschwader* were now assigned to the support of the German offensive south of the Somme. Although compelled to withdraw gradually before the onslaught of ten Panzer divisions, the French fought hard, contesting every yard of ground, and inflicted substantial casualties on the enemy. But the German armour exploited every gap, racing across country and by-passing the strongpoints that had been set up by the French. On several occasions, the tanks advanced so rapidly that they crossed the *Luftwaffe*'s bomb line, with the attendant danger that they might be attacked by their own Ju 87s, and had to be halted while the rest of the offensive caught up.

By nightfall on 13 June, 1940, the French forces in the west – the Seventh and Tenth Armies and the Army of Paris, the latter formed originally to defend the capital to the last – were all in full retreat. The next day, German forces entered Paris, and on the 22nd an armistice brought an end to one of the fastest and most devastating campaigns in the history of warfare.

There is no doubt at all that the Ju 87 Stuka had been a decisive factor in the outcome of that campaign, but that success had come at some cost. Firm figures for Ju 87 losses during the Battle of France are difficult to establish, as *Luftwaffe* records, when referring to dive bomber casualties, do not distinguish between Ju 87 and Ju 88; similarly, when referring to 'assault aircraft' losses, the records make no distinction between Ju 87 and Hs 123. What is known is that on 10 May 1940 the *Luftwaffe* had

This Junkers Ju 87B of III/StG 2, T6+HL, was brought down near the Selsey-Chichester road during an attack on Tangmere aerodrome on 16 August 1940. The pilot and gunner, *Unteroffizier* Koenig and *Unteroffizier* Schmid, were wounded and taken prisoner. (*via Phil Jarrett*)

417 dive bombers of all types on strength, and that of these, 89 were lost to enemy action and 24 on operations but not due to enemy action (in other words, due to factors such as mid-air collisions, of which the Ju 87 suffered a considerable number), making a total of 113. In addition, 28 dive bombers were damaged.

It would, of course, have been a far gloomier picture if the *Stukageschwader* had been faced with strong and determined fighter opposition throughout the campaign. And as the fighting in France came to an end, the martyrdom of the Stukas was only weeks away.

The Battle of Britain

The first Stuka attack on the British Isles was made on 4 July, 1940, by 33 Ju 87Bs of StG 51. Formed in May 1939, this unit, which comprised a single *Gruppe*, had seen action in the Polish campaign and in France, where it operated as part of *Luftflotte* 3. Now, on this Thursday morning, led by *Major* von Klitzing, it swept down on Portland naval base in Dorset and inflicted substantial damage, sinking the auxiliary anti-aircraft vessel HMS *Foylebank* with the loss of 176 lives and damaging several other vessels. One Stuka was shot down and a second badly damaged. Five days later, III/StG 51 was redesignated II/StG 1, and disappeared from the *Luftwaffe* order of battle.

On 9 July Stukas, covered by a fighter escort, appeared over Portland again, 27 aircraft of I/StG 77 from Caen dive-bombing the base. One Ju 87 was shot down by a Spitfire. Another sortie to the Portland area was made on 11 July, when two *Staffeln* of III/StG 2 attacked under an umbrella of Messerschmitt Bf 110s. The latter clashed with RAF fighters and four were shot down; one Ju 87B failed to return. Elsewhere, a convoy off Dover was attacked by Stukas of IV(Stuka)/LG 1, which had one aircraft destroyed and another damaged.

The Stuka units of VIII *Fliegerkorps* had now moved to new locations on the Cherbourg peninsula, from where they were better placed to attack British naval installations in the south-west and the convoys passing along the south coast. The next major action, however, was fought on 13 July off Dover, when eleven Hurricanes of No 56 Squadron encountered a large formation of StG 1 Stukas with a strong fighter escort. The RAF pilots claimed to have destroyed seven Ju 87s, but in fact only two were damaged, these making forced landings on the French coast. The next day, a Ju 87 of IV/LG 1 was shot down off Dover harbour.

Dover harbour itself was the scene of a heavy Stuka attack on 19 July, as was Portland, and in both cases the dive bombers suffered no losses. The following evening, however, Stukas of StG 1 carrying out a convoy attack off Dover were badly mauled by a squadron of Hurricanes, and although none was lost, four crash-landed in France with serious damage.

Continuing Channel action

The Stukas were very active on 25 July, the day beginning with an attack on Portland by aircraft of III/StG 1. One Ju 87B was shot down by fighters and two damaged. During a convoy attack, II/StG 1 lost two aircraft to fighters, and IV/LG 1 lost one. The only Stuka loss during the next three days was an aircraft of StG 77, which failed to return from operations over the Channel, but on 29 July IV/LG 1 lost two aircraft and II/StG 1 one, all in combat with fighters; several others were damaged.

There followed a comparative lull lasting a week. Then, on 8 August, Hurricanes were at the forefront of a furious air battle that developed when large formations of Ju 87s, under strong fighter escort, attacked a 25-ship convoy off the Isle of Wight. One of the Hurricane squadrons involved was No 145 from Westhampnett, led by Squadron Leader J.R.A Peel. The RAF pilots were about to engage a Stuka formation when they were themselves 'bounced' by Bf 109s and forced on the defensive. Two Hurricanes, one of them Peel's, were shot down: Peel was rescued from the sea near Boulogne. The day's fighting cost the RAF fifteen Hurricanes and Spitfires against 21 enemy aircraft destroyed. Eight of the latter were Stukas, three belonging to StG 3 and the rest to StG 77. In addition, nine were damaged, most having to make emergency landings in France. Taking into account the fact that the convoy had suffered the loss of three ships sunk by *Schnellboote*, three more being damaged during a night attack, with eleven more damaged by air attack during the day, it had not been a good time for either side.

Bad weather frustrated air operations on 9

and 10 August, the latter originally scheduled as *Adlertag* – Eagle Day, the start of the air offensive proper – but on 11 August four heavy air attacks were launched on Dover and Portland. IV/LG 1 and II/StG 1 each lost a Ju 87 during the day's operations, both shot down by fighters over the Thames estuary.

At noon on 12 August, a day in which the *Luftwaffe* carried out heavy attacks on Britain's south coast radar stations, the Chain Home Low (CHL) station at Foreness, which was untouched, reported 50 plus hostiles off North Foreland. They were Stukas, and they were searching for two Channel convoys, code-named *Agent* and *Arena*. The attack on the latter was successful, two vessels being damaged by IV/LG 1, but the attack on *Agent* was beaten off, albeit at the cost of four Hurricanes destroyed. All the Ju 87s returned to base.

Eagle Day

Adlertag was launched on Tuesday, 13 August, and got off to a bad start, early operations being disrupted by bad weather. Then, starting at 1500, 52 Ju 87Bs of StG 2 began taking off from their base at Flers to attack airfields in the Portland area. They were escorted by Bf 109s of JG 27. However, southern England was hidden under a blanket of cloud, so making a dive-bombing attack out of the question. The Stukas circled over the coast in search of a target. Within minutes, their fighter escort was being hotly engaged by a strong force of Hurricanes from Exeter and Middle Wallop, while fifteen Spitfires of No 609 Squadron attacked the bombers, causing them to jettison their bombs. Five of the Stukas were quickly shot down, and a sixth crashed near the Channel Islands after catching fire on its way home.

Meanwhile, over Kent, No 11 Group, Fighter Command, was having a hard time. General Bruno Loerzer's II *Fliegerkorps* had sent in both its Stuka units, IV/LG 1 and StG 1, preceded by the Bf 109s of JG 26. The Messerschmitts were able to beat off a flight of Spitfires from Kenley, allowing the 86 Stukas to proceed unmolested to their target, the airfield of Detling near Maidstone. Fifteen minutes later the airfield lay in ruins; the hangars were burning, the operations room was wrecked, the station commander was dead and twenty British

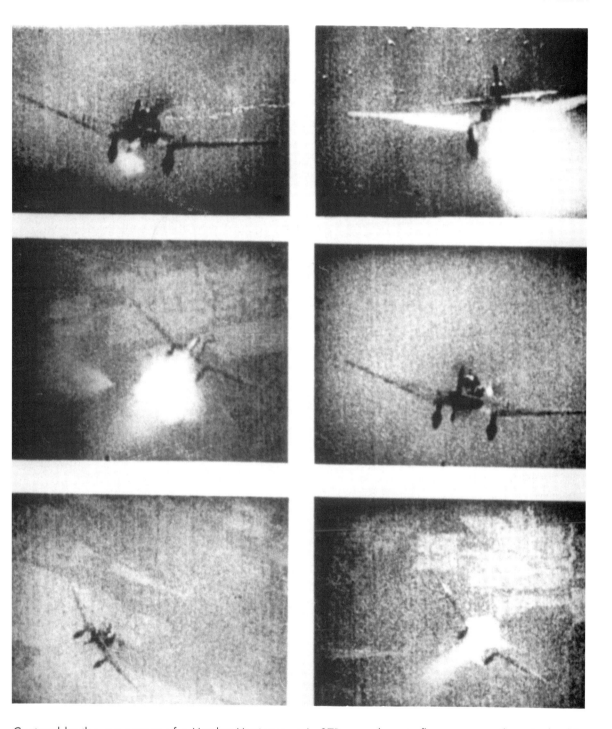

Captured by the gun camera of a Hawker Hurricane, a Ju 87B goes down in flames over southern England in August 1940. The Stukas were most vulnerable when diving: their escorts, lacking dive brakes, quickly plunged away from the ungainly dive bombers, leaving them totally at the mercy of incoming British fighters. (*Author*)

A Ju 87B-2 of IV/StG 2 seen in the summer of 1940. The *Staffel* or squadron emblem was a four-leafed clover superimposed on a white diamond. (*via Phil Jarrett*)

aircraft were destroyed. It was a brilliant attack, and in terms of its execution a highly successful one. But there were no RAF fighters at Detling; it was a Coastal Command station. All the Stukas returned safely to base.

On 14 August, operations against the British Isles were hampered by bad weather, but attacks by small numbers of aircraft on Manston, Dover, Middle Wallop and Sealand cost the *Luftwaffe* eleven bombers and six fighters, including a Stuka of LG 1.

Thursday, 15 August 1940, was the climax of the Battle of Britain, a disastrous day for the *Luftwaffe* that saw the loss of 71 of its aircraft against a Fighter Command loss of 29. While the fighter squadrons of Nos 12 and 13 Groups fought off attacks on northern England by the bombers of *Luftflotte* V, based in Norway and Denmark, heavily-escorted Stukas fell on Hawkinge airfield in 11 Group, inflicting considerable damage. More seriously, bombs severed power to Dover, Rye and Foreness radar stations, blinding them for most of the day. Of the six Stukas shot down on 15 August, three were Ju 87Rs of II/StG 2, engaged in an attack on Portland.

On 16 August the *Luftwaffe* returned in force, again striking at airfields and radar facilities. It was a bad day for the Stukas, StG 2 losing nine aircraft destroyed and six damaged. And there was worse to come. On Sunday, 18 August, following another spell of bad weather, the Germans launched a series of heavy attacks on the sector stations of Kenley and Biggin Hill. These attacks were carried out mainly by the Dornier 17s of KG 76, which, despite their fighter escort, suffered heavily, losing six aircraft with several more damaged. The most fearful loss of the day, however, was sustained by StG 77, which lost eighteen aircraft to RAF fighters, with five damaged. This brought the total Ju 87 combat losses since the air offensive began in July to 59 aircraft, with a further 33 damaged more or less seriously, and with RAF fighter opposition showing no sign of weakening, there was every prospect of the situation becoming still more costly.

It was too high a price to pay. After the debacle of 18 August, 1940, with the exception of some sporadic attacks on Channel convoys later in the year, the Ju 87 played no further part in the Battle of Britain.

3. Operational History 1941-45: Mediterranean and Eastern Front

Beginning on 20 December, 1940, units of *Luftflotte* 2 began transferring from France to bases in Sicily for air operations against the island of Malta, which had been subject to Italian air attack since June. The forces available initially included 53 Ju 87s of I and II/StG 2, together with twelve Ju 87s of StG 1. By the beginning of January 1941 the *Luftwaffe* strength on Italy was 141 aircraft, operating under the command of X *Fliegerkorps*, which had transferred its HQ from Norway.

For two days, beginning on 9 January, the *Regia Aeronautica* and *Fliegerkorps* X mounted heavy attacks on a convoy of four merchant ships sailing from Gibraltar to Malta and escorted by warships of Force H, the Royal Navy's Western Mediterranean task force that included the aircraft carrier HMS *Illustrious*. On 10 January the latter was seriously damaged in a Stuka attack, which also set ablaze the cruiser HMS *Southampton*, later abandoned and sunk by British naval forces. HMS *Illustrious* was hit again later in the day by a Ju 87 of the Italian 237a *Squadriglia*, which had equipped with the Junkers dive bomber in the previous month. From 11 to 19 January, Valletta harbour was subjected to very heavy attacks by Ju 87s and Ju 88s, attempting unsuccessfully to finish off the disabled *Illustrious*. After temporary repairs at Valletta the carrier sailed for the USA to undergo more extensive repair work, and was out of action for several months. Her air group was left behind on Malta, and the Fairey Fulmars of No 806 Squadron took part in the defence of the island until March, when they embarked on the carrier HMS *Formidable*.

Following these attacks, no further supplies reached the island – which was under almost constant air attack – until the last week in March, when a small convoy of four ships was sent through from Alexandria. Two of the ships and the precious stores they carried were damaged by bombs while unloading. The situation was critical, and was only saved when the Stuka units on Italy were withdrawn to take part in the Balkans campaign, leaving the Italians to maintain the siege of Malta alone.

North Africa

Meanwhile, in February 1941, units of the newly-formed *Deutsches Afrika Korps* (DAK) had become established in North Africa. Under the command of General Erwin Rommel, the initial German buildup in the theatre was supported by about 110 aircraft. These included the He 111s of II/KG 26, which had been operating from Benghazi since mid-January, and a *Gruppe* of StG 1, equipped with Ju 87Rs. Also deployed were the Messerschmitt Bf 110s of ZG 26, earmarked for escort duty. In July, the German Stuka units in North Africa were joined by the Italian 209a *Squadriglia* (96 *Gruppo*), equipped with Ju 87Bs.

Based in Tripolitania, the German Stukas were first sent into action against the town of El Agheila, which had been captured from the Italians by the British in February. On 31 March, all Stuka units were assigned to the support of Rommel's offensive towards the vital port of Tobruk. British Commonwealth forces,

British aircraft in flames at Takali airstrip after a Stuka attack. (*Author*)

depleted by the demands of the Greek campaign, were soon in retreat. By 15 April, Tobruk had been surrounded and Axis forces had crossed the Egyptian frontier at Halfaya. At this time, again because of the redeployment of squadrons to Greece, British air strength in Cyrenaica had been reduced to three squadrons of Hawker Hurricanes and one of Bristol Blenheims, supported by three squadrons of Vickers Wellingtons operating from bases in the Suez Canal Zone and one from Malta.

One of the Hurricane squadrons, No 73, was given the task of defending Tobruk. Ranged alongside it was a flight of No 6 Squadron, also with Hurricanes, acting in the army-co-operation role. No 6 Squadron was kept very busy during the battle for Tobruk, as it was the only artillery co-operation unit within the perimeter. The squadron war diary reflects the grimness of the situation:

"May 2nd-6th. These last few days have been eventful in the extreme; so much so that looking back on them, it is almost impossible to put the various happenings in their right order or even to allot them to their right days. We have had intermittent shelling; worse still, we have been ground strafed several times, and on one very unpleasant occasion we were attacked by twenty-two dive bombers with such fierceness and accuracy that we were on the road to believing that the German airmen had a personal grudge against us... It is becoming increasingly difficult to operate. Our serviceability has dwindled to such an extent that, at the moment, we have only one machine that is flyable, and that won't change [propeller] pitch and can, therefore, only take to the air for ten minutes."

Such was to remain the pattern over events in besieged Tobruk during the interminable weeks to come.

War in the Balkans

The Balkans campaign had crippled British strength in North Africa. On 28 October, 1940, Italian forces invaded Greece from Albania, which Italy had overrun in April 1939. Great Britain was obliged to contribute to the defence

38

A Vickers Wellington bomber lies wrecked in its blast pen after a heavy air attack on Malta. (*Author*)

of the Balkan countries in the event of such an invasion, and although the Greek government declined an offer of British ground forces for fear of provoking a German reaction, the British offer of air support was eagerly accepted, and with its help the Greeks fought the Italians to a standstill.

German intervention

Then, on 6 April 1941 27 German divisions, of which seven were armoured, struck simultaneously in eastern Macedonia and Yugoslavia, in part to rescue Mussolini from his problems, but also to secure the southern flank in preparation for the planned invasion of Russia, which was now only weeks away. Although the Yugoslav capital, Belgrade, was declared an open city, it was attacked by the Ju 87s of Richthofen's VIII *Fliegerkorps*, which inflicted heavy damage. The Stukas, belonging to I/StG 1, I/StG 2 and I/StG 77, operated from bases in western Romania as an integral part of *Luftflotte* IV. Over the next fortnight, until the Yugoslav government capitulated, they

operated as they had done before, attacking airfields and enemy ground forces.

After seizing their principal objectives in Yugoslavia, the Germans launched an all-out offensive in Greece, where British Commonwealth troops had now been committed. The overwhelming air superiority enjoyed by the Germans soon became apparent as the Stukas quickly established themselves on forward airstrips; on 14 April they inflicted heavy casualties on the Australian and New Zealand Army Corps (ANZAC), and continued to harass the retreating Allied forces while suffering minimal losses. Faced with this overwhelming superiority, it was not long before the RAF commander in Greece, Air Vice-Marshal J.H. D'Albiac, had to withdraw what remained of his effective strength to the Athens area to provide air cover for an inevitable evacuation. This got under way on 24 April, and in the next five days, under constant air attack by *Luftflotte* 4, the Royal Navy succeeded in embarking 50,672 troops and transporting them to Crete and Egypt.

A Maltese soldier stands guard over the wreck of a Ju 87, shot down over the island by Hurricanes. (*Author*)

Meanwhile, in Egypt, the British Eighth Army, under heavy pressure from the Axis forces, was in urgent need of reinforcements, with particular reference to tanks and aircraft. Between 5 and 25 May, therefore, Force H and the Mediterranean Fleet mounted a joint operation, code-named *Tiger*, to push a convoy of five fast merchantmen carrying the necessary equipment through the Mediterranean from Gibraltar to Alexandria. The convoy passed Gibraltar on 6 May and was escorted by Force H to a point south of Malta, where it was covered by destroyers and cruisers from the island base until it could be met by a strong force sent out from Alexandria. On 8 May, the convoy, sailing in two groups, was detected by enemy air reconnaissance and was attacked initially by Italian SM79 bombers, followed by Ju 87s escorted by Bf 110s. The attacks were broken up by Fairey Fulmar fighters from the carrier HMS *Formidable*, and no damage was inflicted in the ships, although one transport was sunk by mines and another damaged. During the passage of the convoy Stukas of

II/StG 2, led by *Leutnant* Rieger, attempted to dive-bomb the ships at night, but the attack was unsuccessful.

Airborne invasion of Crete

On 20 May 1941, in the wake of a massive air bombardment, German airborne forces landed on Crete (Operation *Merkur*). The next morning the *Luftwaffe* launched the first of a series of heavy attacks on British warships in the area, sinking the destroyer *Juno* and damaging the cruiser *Ajax*. During the night of 21/22 May the Germans attempted to send in reinforcements by sea, but the convoy was attacked by British warships and scattered. A second convoy was also attacked, but the British warships came under constant air attack by the Ju 88s of LG 1 and KG 30 and the Do 17s of KG 2, so they succeeded in destroying only two transports. Two British cruisers, *Carlisle* and *Naiad*, were damaged by bomb hits.

The Royal Navy suffered heavily on the afternoon of 22 May. The fleet came under attack by the Ju 87s of *Oberstleutnant* Oskar

Stukas attacking an anti-aircraft battery on Malta, April 1941. (*Author*)

Stukas deployed to North Africa were initially escorted by Messerschmitt Bf 110s of ZG 26 'Horst Wessel'. This one fell victim to a Hurricane. (*Author*)

A Ju 87B of II/StG 77 in flight over the Balkans during the German offensive in 1941. German aircraft in service in the various operational areas carried distinctive theatre markings: in the Mediterranenan they were distinguished by yellow noses and/or tails. (*Via Phil Jarrett*)

Dinort's StG 2, the Ju 88s of LG 1, Bf 109 fighter-bombers of III/JG 77 and, to a lesser extent, by Italian high-level bombers. The battleship HMS *Warspite* was hit several times by III/JG 77, the cruiser *Gloucester* and the destroyer *Greyhound* were sunk under the combined onslaught of Ju 87s and Ju 88s, and the cruiser *Fiji* was so badly hit by the dive bombers that she had to be abandoned. The cruisers *Carlisle* and *Naiad* suffered further damage, and the battleship *Valiant* was also hit.

On 23 May, Stukas of I/StG 2, led by *Hauptmann* Hitschhold, located the destroyers *Kashmir* and *Kelly* and sank both of them shortly before nightfall; 279 survivors were picked up. On 25 May, Vice-Admiral H.D. Pridham-Wippell put to sea from Alexandria with the battleships *Barham* and *Queen Elizabeth* and nine destroyers. Their aim was to attack the enemy airfield at Scarpanto, which was occupied by the Ju 87s of III/StG 2. Returning from this sortie on the 26th, *Formidable* and the

destroyer *Nubian* were both badly damaged in an attack by Stukas of II/StG 2, and the next day *Barham* was also damaged by Ju 88s.

By this time, it was clear that the situation on Crete was untenable. The harbour at Suda Bay was being so heavily bombed that it was no longer possible to run in supplies and reinforcements. Without air cover, British naval forces were certain to suffer unacceptable losses in their efforts to prevent seaborne landings on the island, a mission that could in any case not be guaranteed. In the afternoon of 27 May, therefore, the British War Cabinet decided to evacuate the garrison of some 32,000 troops, and on the night of 28/29 May, 4700 were embarked at Heraklion and Sfakia. During this operation the destroyer *Imperial* was damaged by air attack and had to be abandoned. She was later sunk by the destroyer *Hotspur*. Another 6000 troops were evacuated on the next night, but during the day Stukas of III/StG 2 sank the destroyer *Hereward* and damaged the cruisers

Junkers Ju 87s on an airfield in Greece. In 1941, the Allies had nothing to compare with the Ju 87 as a tactical support aircraft. The Stuka's fearsome reputation meant that its very appearance overhead followed by the banshee wail of its siren as it dived struck terror into the hearts of its enemies. (*via Phil Jarrett*)

A Ju 87R-1, equipped with long-range tanks, over Greece. Known as the *Richard*, the aircraft needed to have an extended range in order to operate against Crete from bases on the Greek mainland. (*via Phil Jarrett*)

Ajax, *Dido* and *Orion*, as well as the destroyer *Decoy*. *Orion* suffered terrible casualties among the troops she was carrying; of the 1100 soldiers on board, 260 were killed and 280 were wounded.

On the night of 31 May/1 June the Royal Navy sent in the fast cruiser/minelayer *Abdiel*, accompanied by the destroyers *Hotspur*, *Jackal* and *Kimberley*, in a last attempt to evacuate at least some of the 6000 troops assembled at Sfakia. In a herculean effort, the destroyers lifted off 4000 men before the onset of dawn brought an end to the operation; the destroyers then headed for Alexandria, and the cruisers *Calcutta* and *Coventry* were dispatched to meet them. These two warships, however, were located to the north of Alexandria by two Ju 88s, which dive-bombed and sank the *Calcutta*; 255 survivors were rescued by the other cruiser.

The Royal Navy had succeeded in evacuating 17,000 troops from Crete, but 15,743 had been killed or captured. In addition, the Navy had lost 2011 personnel. German casualties had not been light, either; losses amounted to 6580 dead, wounded or missing. Never again would the Germans attempt a major airborne assault.

In addition to the human loss, the battle for Crete had cost the Royal Navy three cruisers and six destroyers, with two battleships, an aircraft carrier, six cruisers and seven destroyers sustaining varying degrees of damage. As a demonstration of the superiority of air power over naval might, nothing could have been more convincing; and it was the Ju 87 Stuka that had been at the forefront.

Operation *Barbarossa*

With their southern flank secure, and Erwin Rommel showing every sign of reaching the Suez Canal in Egypt, the Germans launched Operation *Barbarossa*, the long-planned attack on the Soviet Union, on 22 June 1941. The invasion was supported by four *Luftflotten*, with *Luftflotte* 4 supporting Army Group South.

Seven *Stukagruppen* were placed at the disposal of II and VIII *Fliegerkorps*: II/ and III/StG 1 with 70 aircraft, I/ and III/StG 2 with 83 aircraft, and the whole of StG 77 with 122 aircraft. In addition, IV/LG I was operational in northern Norway with 42 Ju 87Bs. Throughout the first day of the invasion, which caught the Soviet High Command completely unwares, Soviet airfields and other installations were

Above: Stukas of StG 2 seen over northern Russia in October 1941 as they return, weaponless, from a mission. (*via Phil Jarrett*)

Below: A Ju 87B, dive brakes extended, begins its plunge towards a target somewhere in the vast expanse of the Soviet Union. (*via Phil Jarrett*)

subjected to heavy attacks by 800 bombers and dive bombers, supported by 440 Messerschmitt Bf 109s and 40 Bf 110s. Soviet losses in the day's operations were 1489 aircraft destroyed on the ground and 322 in the air; the *Luftwaffe*'s loss was 35, including three Ju 87s. It was the greatest victory ever achieved in a single day by one air force over another.

During these early operations, II/ and III/StG 1 came under the command of VIII *Fliegerkorps*, supporting Army Group Centre; in September, III *Gruppe* was sent to north Russia to operate under the orders of I *Fliegerkorps*. I *Gruppe* remained in the Mediterranean theatre. II/StG 2 was also in the Mediterranean theatre during this period, having moved from Sicily to North Africa, while I and III *Gruppe*n operated as part of VIII *Fliegerkorps* in support of Army Group Centre until late August. They then redeployed to the Leningrad front for intensive operations against lines of communication between Moscow and Leningrad under *Luftflotte* 1 command. The other *Stuka-geschwader*, StG 77, operated under the orders of

Ju 87B-2 NO+HP of III/StG 2 seen after nosing over on muddy ground at Prague-Ruzyne in November 1941. The Stuka was prone to such unwanted manoeuvres if its pilots did not take care. (*via Phil Jarrett*)

II *Fliegerkorps* in support of Army Group Centre until September, when it moved south for operations in the Crimea as part of *Luftflotte* 4. On 21-22 September, StG 77 was heavily engaged in attacking warships supporting a Soviet amphibious landing designed to eliminate Romanian coastal batteries near Grigorevka. The Stukas sank the Soviet destroyer *Frunze* and the gunboat *Krasnaya Armeniya*. On the following day, the dive bombers badly damaged the destroyer *Besposhchadny*, which had to be towed into harbour stern first, and damaged a second destroyer, *Bezuprechny*, with near-misses. The former was to be sunk by air attack at Sevastopol in October 1943, and the latter would also be destroyed at Yalta in June 1942.

Baltic anti-ship missions

Meanwhile, I/ and III/StG 2 had begun operations against the Soviet Baltic Fleet at Kronshtadt and Leningrad. On 21 September a Stuka of III/StG 2 flown by *Lt* Hans-Ulrich Rudel hit the battleship *Marat* with a 1000kg (2204lb) bomb, demolishing the warship's bow. The *Marat* settled on the harbour bottom, where she remained for the rest of the war, although her main armament was still operational. She was refloated in 1946 and used for some time as a gunnery training ship. The cruiser *Kirov* was also attacked by *Hauptmann* Steen, commander of III/StG 2; his aircraft was hit by AA fire and fell into the sea, its pilot having made a desperate but vain attempt to steer it into the cruiser, which was damaged by the explosion of the Stuka's bomb. In other attacks, the battleship *Oktyabrskaya Revolutsiya* managed to escape severe damage, but took hits from six medium bombs.

The intense air bombardment was maintained for a period of three days, in the course of which the destroyer *Steregushchi* capsized after a direct hit. She was later salvaged. The destroyers *Gordy*, *Grozyaschi* and *Silny* were damaged, along with the submarine depot ship *Smolny* and the submarine Shch-306. On 23 September the cruiser *Maksim Gorki*, already hit during an attack on Leningrad, was damaged again, as was the cruiser *Kirov* and the destroyer *Grozyashch*i off Kronshtadt. The submarine P.2 was destroyed in the dockyard, and the flotilla leader *Minsk* sank after a direct hit. She too was later salvaged. The patrol ship *Taifun* was destroyed, and the submarine Shch-302 damaged.

In mid-November the Germans, having

The Ju 87B-1/Trop was issued to attack squadrons of the Italian *Regia Aeronautica* from late 1940, and was operated by the 96th, 97th, 101st and 121st *Gruppi Tuffatori*. They saw considerable action in the Balkans and in North Africa and were heavily involved in Axis attacks against Malta. (*via Phil Jarrett*)

An Italian Ju 87B-1/Trop in North Africa. Italian Stukas usually kept the standard *Luftwaffe* colour scheme of *Schwarzgrun* 70 (black green) upper surfaces and *Hellblau* 65 (light blue) under surfaces, onto which were painted Italian national markings. (*via Phil Jarrett*)

taken 700,000 Russian prisoners in the preceding three weeks, launched the second phase of their offensive. This was an attempt to encircle Moscow from the Tula and Kalinin areas, but very slow progress was made. The Russian winter was now in its early stages, hampering operations in the air and on the ground.

Mediterranean Theatre 1941-43

Following the departure of *Luftwaffe* units from Sicily to take part in the Balkan and Russian campaigns, attacks on the island of Malta and its supply convoys became the exclusive task of the *Regia Aeronautica* until December 1941, when, as a preliminary to neutralizing Malta as a strategic base, the *Luftwaffe* returned to Sicily with II *Fliegerkorps*. This comprised I/KG 54, II/ and III/KG 77, *Küstenfliegergruppe* (KGr) 606 and KGr 806, all with Junkers Ju 88A-4s; I/ and III/StG 3 with Ju 87s; I/NJG 2 with Ju 88C night intruders; III/ZG 26 with Messerschmitt Bf 110s; and JG 53 with Bf 109Fs.

Initially, the bombers carried out dispersed dive-bombing attacks in small groups and

suffered substantial losses, but by the end of the year II *Fliegerkorps* had worked out a revised bombing policy. The aim, which the Germans would attempt to implement early in 1942, was threefold. First, to destroy the RAF fighter defences on Malta by means of heavy and repeated air attacks; second, to neutralize the bomber and torpedo-bomber bases on the island; and third, to attack the docks and harbour installations around Valletta. When these objectives were acheved, the island would be open to invasion.

In North Africa, in June 1941, the strength of the *Regia Aeronautica* stood at 70 fighters and 25 bombers. The fighter units were the 2*o* and 155*o* groups with Fiat G.50s and the 18*o* and 151*o* with Fiat CR.42s, while two groups of the 43*o* *Stormo* had Fiat BR.20s for night bombing. In July this force was joined by the 153*o* and 157*o* *Gruppi* with Macchi MC.200s, and the 209*a* *Squadriglia* with Junkers Ju 87Bs. The *Luftwaffe* forces in North Africa were still relatively small, the principal bomber force comprising the Ju 87s of II/StG 2 and I/StG 3; detachments of Bf 110s for escort duty were rotated from Greece,

This Ju 87B was based in Sicily in 1941, during the siege of Malta. The fuselage code indicates that it was probably attached to StG 77. (*via Phil Jarrett*)

Ju 87Bs of I/StG 2 lined up on an airfield in Sicily. Note the 'Scottie' terrier badge that was the emblem of the *Gruppe's* 1.*Staffel.* (*via Phil Jarrett*)

A Junkers Ju 87D-3 of III/*Stukageschwader* 3, captured by the British in North Africa and used as a 'hack' by No 213 Squadron. Below can be seen the same aircraft after being repainted in RAF markings – although the swastika is only partly obscured by the fin flash. (*via Phil Jarrett*)

and it was not until the late summer of 1941 that the Air Commander Africa (*Fliegerführer Afrika*) received adequate fighter protection for his dive bombers in the form of the first echelons of JG 27, the old and trusted Stuka escort *Geschwader*, with Bf 109Fs.

Although lacking adequate fighter escort at the time, the Axis dive bomber squadrons played a considerable role in halting Operation *Battleaxe*, which was launched in June 1941 by British and Empire forces in an attempt to break

Rommel's hold on Cyrenaica and relieve Tobruk. The failure of the offensive underlined the need for effective air-ground co-operation, something which the British had not developed to a satisfactory degree at this stage. It had improved by November 1941, when the British launched Operation *Crusader*; this had the multiple aims of destroying the bulk of Rommel's armour, relieving Tobruk and retaking Cyrenaica as a preliminary to invading Tripolitania. The offensive enjoyed initial success, although an attempted breakout by the Tobruk garrison was forestalled by the rapid deployment of Rommel's armour, strongly supported by the German and Italian Stuka units. The German defensive line at Gazala was breached in December and British forces pushed on towards Benghazi, but were halted at El Agheila.

Meanwhile, the Stukas of the Sicily-based III/StG 3, which was now in the process of rearming with the improved Ju 87D-1 model, continued to pound Malta and its supply convoys. Attacks on the island's airfields continued in January and February 1942, although these were hampered by bad weather. An attempt to supply Malta from Alexandria with the aid of three fast merchantmen on 12 February failed, two being sunk and one disabled.

Spitfires delivered to Malta

On 7 March 1942 the first Spitfires reached Malta, flown in at enormous risk from the carrier HMS *Eagle*. A fortnight later the *Luftwaffe* launched a massive onslaught aimed at the destruction of Malta's dwindling fighter force, beginning with an attack by 60 Ju 88s on Takali airfield. Takali was again heavily bombed by Ju 87s and Ju 88s the next day. On 22 March four supply ships, escorted by four light cruisers and 16 destroyers, attempted to reach Malta from Alexandria. An attempt by Italian warships to intercept the convoy was beaten off in the Gulf of Sirte, but the ships were later subjected to heavy air attack. The transport *Clan Campbell* was sunk 32 km (20 miles) short of the island and the naval supply ship *Breconshire* was so badly damaged that she had to be beached. The other two transports reached Valletta harbour, but both were sunk by air attack two days later. Only one-fifth of the convoy's supplies reached Malta's storehouses.

On 20 April 1942 the American carrier USS *Wasp*, having sailed from the Clyde via Gibraltar, flew off 54 Spitfires for Malta, of which 47 reached the island. By the end of the next day, under repeated air attack, only 18 remained airworthy. Then, on 11 May, the USS *Wasp* and HMS *Eagle* jointly flew off 64 more Spitfires for Malta, of which 60 reached the

Down in the desert: A Ju 87 comes to grief near Tobruk after being attacked by Allied fighters in 1941. The Stukas were usually escorted by the Messerschmitt Bf 109s of JG 27. (*via Phil Jarrett*)

island safely. Although Malta's ordeal was far from over, these reinforcements enabled the RAF to establish air superiority over the island for the first time, permitting the deployment of torpedo-bomber squadrons which, in the second half of the year, would wreak havoc on Rommel's supply lines.

On 9 May, III/StG 3 made its last attack on Malta, losing several aircraft to AA fire and Spitfires. A few days later the Stukas departed for North Africa, and by 20 May the whole *Geschwader*, equipped with a mixture of Ju 87D-1s and Ju 87Rs, was established at Bir el Hania.

The period between March and May 1942 witnessed a developing struggle for air superiority in North Africa, as a preliminary to Rommel's planned summer offensive. On 26 May, reinforced by the Stukas from Sicily, the Afrika Korps launched a fierce assault on the

Something of a mystery surrounds this Italian Ju 87B, which apparently ran out of fuel and overturned while attempting to land in British-held territory. A scrawled message in the cockpit indicated that the crew had survived; they had presumably wandered off into the desert. (*via Phil Jarrett*)

British-held Gazala Line, which consisted of a series of 'Brigade Boxes' strongly supported by artillery and protected by minefields. At the start of the battle the Desert Air Force had 290 serviceable combat aircraft, compared to the German and Italian total of 497. From 1 to 10 June, all squadrons of the Desert Air Force were committed to the support of Free French forces holding the fort of Bir Hacheim, at the southern end of the Gazala Line, which was under heavy attack by the Stukas of StG 3. On 10 June, utterly exhausted, the surviving Frenchmen fought their way out of Bir Hacheim, their fierce resistance having bought a ten-day respite that prevented Rommel from outflanking the British positions and driving on to Cairo. Instead, the Eighth Army fell back to new defensive positions at El Alamein, where Rommel's drive into Egypt was halted.

On 14 and 15 June, the full fury of the Africa-based Stukas – those of StG 3 and the Italian 102o *Gruppo* from Tunisia – was turned against a Malta convoy code-named *Harpoon*. This consisted of six large merchant ships and an escort that included the carriers HMS *Eagle* and HMS *Argus*. The convoy's fighter cover comprised 16 Sea Hurricanes and a small number of Fulmars, which claimed to have destroyed eleven enemy aircraft by the end of the first day, with many others damaged and driven off. On 15 June, however, the carrier support force turned back for Gibraltar, leaving the convoy dependent on Malta-based fighter cover. Only two of the merchant vessels reached the island. A second convoy from Alexandria, menaced by the Italian fleet, was forced to turn back.

Assault on Tobruk

On 20 June 1942, operating from the newly-captured forward airstrips of Gambut and El Adem, the *Luftwaffe* and *Regia Aeronautica* launched a massive air assault on the defences of Tobruk, the Germans flying 580 sorties and the Italians 177 on this one day. The Stukas' initial objectives were the minefields to the southeast of Tobruk, their bombs opening up gaps that were exploited by the German and Italian infantry. Later, the Stukas turned their attention to precision targets such as gun batteries and strongpoints. Unable to withstand the combined air and ground onslaught, the Tobruk garrison surrendered on 21 June. Only two Stukas were lost during the entire

A Stuka of the *Regia Aeronautica* preparing for take-off, November 1942. This photograph gives a good impression of the dive-bomber's size – which was very large for a single-engined machine. (via Phil Jarrett)

operation, both as the result of a collision.

The continual air operations of June 1942 – the assault on Bir Hacheim, the attacks on the Malta convoys, the bombardment of Tobruk – combined with a shortage of fuel and the effects of heavy sandstorms greatly reduced Axis aircraft serviceability at this critical juncture. Rommel pushed on towards Egypt with severely depleted air cover, and as a result the Allies were able to intensify their air attacks on the Axis forces during July, delaying the enemy advance and enabling the Eighth Army to strengthen its positions at El Alamein.

Having held off the DAK during the summer, the British, under their new commander, General Bernard L. Montgomery, used the Alamein position to mount a massive offensive against the Axis forces at the end of October. The busiest day of air operations during the Battle of Alamein was 3 November 1942. On the Axis side, the Germans flew 1550 sorties and lost 64 aircraft, while the Italians lost about 20 in an estimated 1570 sorties. Then, on 8 November, British and American forces began landing in Algeria. Faced with fighting on two fronts the Axis forces were soon in full retreat towards Tunisia. As the Eighth Army's advance rolled across North Africa from east to west, the Desert Air Force maintained the air superiority it had won before Alamein, mounting continual attacks on the enemy convoys that jammed the coast roads leading through Cyrenaica. In northwest Africa, however, the situation in the air was different.

A Ju 87D carrying a cluster of fragmentation bombs under each wing. Stukas carrying such armament were deadly weapons against troop concentrations and unarmoured vehicles. (*via Phil Jarrett*)

Here, handicapped by a lack of suitable airfields that forced their aircraft to operate at ever-growing distances from the front line, the Allies suffered heavily; the *Luftwaffe* enjoyed superiority in the battlefield area. By the end of November 1942, *Luftwaffe* units in northwest Africa were beginning to receive the Focke-Wulf Fw 190, mostly the G-1 ground attack version. The first unit to equip was II/*Schlachtgeschwader* 2 at Zarzun, Tunisia.

The end in Africa

On 15 January, 1943, when the Allies launched the first of a series of offensives that would utimately lead to the collapse of the Axis cause in North Africa, German ground attack forces comprised II/ and III/StG 3 with the Ju 87D-1/Trop, I/SchG 2 with similar equipment, and 8.SchG 2, a *staffel* equipped with the Henschel Hs 129B. Losses in combat with Allied fighters were severe, however, and by the beginning of May all *Luftwaffe* units had been withdrawn to Sicily, Italy, the Balkans and Sardinia. StG 3 was among the first to leave, being withdrawn to Yugoslavia in March; from there, I *Gruppe* was initially assigned to *Luftflotte* 4 in southern Russia, III *Gruppe* went to support Army Group Centre, and II *Gruppe* went to Greece in July. It

was joined by I *Gruppe* shortly afterwards, both being under the command of X *Fliegerkorps*.

Eastern Front, 1942-1945

In February 1942, IV(Stuka)/LG 1, operating with Ju 87Bs from Kirkenes in northern Norway, was redesignated I/StG 5. Under the command of *Major* Karl Stepp, the *Gruppe* flew intensively against the Murmansk railway, along which supplies from the Allied Arctic convoys were beginning to flow. In December 1942, the unit was transferred to Alakurtii, Finland, for operations in Karelia. In the summer of 1943 it was absorbed into StG 1.

Elsewhere, all three *Gruppen* of StG 3 were operating in southern Russia, concentrating in the Crimea from June under the command of VIII *Fliegerkorps*. In September 1942, III *Gruppe* was transferred north to Bobruisk, from where it operated under the orders of StG 1. Part of the latter had been pulled out of the line for a rest in January 1942, *Stab*.StG 1 and 6.*Staffel* going to Swabisch-Hall, and III *Gruppe* to Schweinfurt. I *Gruppe* was still operating in the Mediterranean, and only II *Gruppe* remained fully operational on the Eastern Front. By July 1942, however, the whole *Geschwader* was again in action against the Russians.

Stukas of I/StG 2 over Russia. StG 2 'Immelmann' operated successfully against the Soviet Fleet. (*via Phil Jarrett*)

I *Gruppe* of StG 2 was also being rested at Neukuhren early in 1942, the Staff Flight and III *Gruppe* remaining operational on the Eastern Front, with II *Gruppe* in the Mediterranean. By the summer of 1942, the entire *Geschwader* was concentrated in southern Russia, under the command of *Luftflotte* 4.

All three *Geschwader* took part in the German onslaught against Stalingrad. The first major air attack on the city took place on 23 August 1942, when 200 bombers of *Luftflotte* 4, escorted by 50 Bf 109s, made the first of a series of raids that lasted all day, the *Luftwaffe* flying some 2,000 sorties. By the middle of September the Germans were fighting in Stalingrad itself, the Stukas lending valuable support wherever possible by carrying out precision attacks on enemy targets. However, as time went by, the fighting in the city became so confused that such attacks were impossible. In the early stages of the battle, however, VIII *Fliegerkorps*

established a field HQ in the German-held western part of Stalingrad, next to an army observation post and command centre, so it was usually possible to call down flights of patrolling Stukas to deal with Soviet artillery positions. The Russians counter-attacked in strength in November, compelling the various units of StG 2, which had been operating from forward airstrips, to carry out a hurried evacuation. Some Stukas continued to operate from within the Stalingrad pocket until December, when they too were forced to evacuate. Attempts to resupply the trapped Germans by air failed; the remnants of the Sixth Army fought on until February, when they were forced to surrender.

Early in 1943 the *Stukageschwader* in Russia underwent some reorganization. In north Russia, *Stab* and III/StG 1 were under the command of *Luftflotte* 1; I *Gruppe* was non-operational, while II *Gruppe* was at Rostov-on-

A Ju 87D-5 over Russia, 1944. The aircraft's national markings have been obliterated by the temporary 'snow camouflage', which was hastily applied with the onset of winter. (*via Phil Jarrett*)

Don. In April, *Stab*, II and III *Gruppen* were assigned to support Army Group Centre. *Stab* and II/StG 2 were also re-forming at Rostov in February 1943, recovering from the mauling they had received at Stalingrad; III *Gruppe* was operating with *Luftwaffenkommando* Don, while I *Gruppe* was under the orders of *Luftflotte* 4 in southern Russia. StG 3 was still in the throes of withdrawing from North Africa; StG 5 (formerly IV (Stuka)/LG 1) was in Finland; and StG 77 was in southern Russia, the whole *Geschwader* becoming established at Bobruisk in May. The air units in south-central Russia now came under the command of *Luftflotte* 6, which had been established by redesignating the former *Luftwaffenkommando Ost*.

The majority of the Stuka units were now armed with the Ju 87D-3 variant, which among other refinements incorporated additional armour protection. Another Stuka variant introduced on the Eastern Front early in 1943, albeit on an experimental basis, was the Ju 87G, which was basically a D-3 equipped with two 37-mm Flak 18 anti-tank cannon. The concept had been tested by veteran Stuka pilot Hans-Ulrich Rudel at Rechlin in January, and a trials unit under the command of *Oberstleutnant* Otto Weiss was soon deployed to the Eastern Front. Later, Rudel was to achieve enormous success with the tank-busting Ju 87G.

Losses to fighters

Although the Stuka could give a good account of itself against attacking fighters, especially when a Ju 87 formation was able to form a defensive circle, the growing proficiency of Soviet fighter pilots and the appearance of new fighter types brought about a sharp increase in losses during 1943. On 22 May, for example, a formation of Ju 87s dive-bombing marshalling yards at Kursk was attacked by Soviet fighters and nine Ju 87s were destroyed. There was an even more remarkable example of the Stuka's vulnerability a few weeks later, when Guards Lieutenant A.K. Gorovets, making skilful use of cloud cover, attacked a formation of Stukas single-handed on 6 July and destroyed nine before he was shot down. He was made a posthumous Hero of the Soviet Union.

This incident occurred during the Battle of Kursk, the last major German offensive on the Eastern Front. A lull in the fighting during the

A Ju 87G-1 runs up its engine prior to a sortie against Soviet armour. Note the Russian T-34 marking on the engine cowling, indicating a tank kill. *(via Phil Jarrett)*

spring had left the Soviet Central and Voronezh Fronts in a potentially dangerous situation, with two German salients at Orel and Kursk flanking a deep bulge to the west of Kursk. In this bulge the Russians had concentrated twelve armies, including two elite Guards and two tank armies. If the Germans could smash their way through the Russian defences to the north and south of Kursk, they would split the Soviet front in two, cutting off all the Russian forces in the salient and destroying them. If the German plan succeeded, the Red Army would have little hope of recovering from such a shattering defeat.

The offensive, code-named Operation *Citadel*, was launched on 5 July 1943. Ground attack forces in support comprised the whole of StG 2 and StG 77, plus III/StG 3, all with the Ju 87D; I

and II/*Schlachtgeschwader* 1 (SchG 1) with the Focke-Wulf Fw 190, and 8.SchG 2 with the Henschel Hs 129B. Two anti-tank *staffeln*, PzJ.Sta/StG 1 and PzJ.Sta/StG 2, formed out of Otto Weiss's trials unit, were armed with the Ju 87G-1 anti-tank aircraft.

Aircraft versus tank

The Battle of Kursk was the first occasion on which aircraft operated in strength against armour, and the air assault that accompanied the German land attack was extremely effective, as recorded in the war diary of the reconnaissance detachment of the Army's elite Grossdeutschland division:

"With admiration we watch the Stukas attacking the Russian tanks uninterruptedly and with wonderful precision. Squadron after

Mechanics at work on a Stuka at an advanced airstrip in Russia. (*via Phil Jarrett*)

squadron of Stukas come over to drop their deadly eggs on the Russian armour. Dazzling white flames indicate that another enemy tank has 'brewed up.' This happens again and again."

Hans-Ulrich Rudel, flying a cannon-armed Ju 87G of StG 2, recalled in his book *Stuka Pilot*:

"In the first attack four tanks explode under the hammer-blows of my cannon; by the evening the total rises to twelve... the evil spell is broken, and in this aircraft we possess a weapon which can speedily be employed everywhere and is capable of dealing successfully with the formidable numbers of Soviet tanks."

Despite the massive air support, however, the German offensive ground to a standstill against stiffening Soviet resistance and ended in failure. From the summer of 1943, German forces in the east were condemned to fight a defensive battle that would ultimately end at the gates of Berlin.

One of the many Stuka aircrew casualties of the Battle of Kursk was *Hauptmann* Walter Krauss, commander of III/StG 2 'Immelmann', killed in a Russian night air raid. His place was taken by Hans-Ulrich Rudel, who continued to lead the *Gruppe* on the Eastern Front during the remainder of the war, and whose achievements are recorded in Chapter 4.

On 5 October, 1943, the *Luftwaffe*'s ground attack forces were reorganized. All dive bomber, ground attack and fast bomber groups were incorporated into new ground attack wings designated *Schlachtgeschwader* (SG). III/StG 2 therefore became III/SG 2. In addition to the German Ju 87 units, Stukas were also operated on the Eastern Front by the 3rd and 6th Dive Bomber Wings of the Royal Romanian Air Force, the 102/1 Dive Bomber Squadron of the Royal Hungarian Air Force, and the Bulgarian and Slovakian Air Forces.

Close support missions were increasingly being flown by the Focke-Wulf Fw 190, and

Stukas in formation over the Russian steppes. (*via Phil Jarrett*)

Stuka units began converting to the type in some numbers. Apart from Rudel's tank-busters, the remaining Ju 87s on the Eastern Front now operated mainly at night in the harassing role. This tactic, pioneered by the Russians with their little Polikarpov Po-2 biplanes, had been adopted by the Germans late in 1942 with the formation of so-called *Storkampfstaffeln*, and in December that year a special *Nachtschlachtgruppe*, NSGr 2, was formed in Italy on the orders of Wolfram von Richthofen. Equipped initially with Fiat CR.42 biplanes, it later acquired a *staffel* of Ju 87s, which saw action against the Allied landings on Sicily in July 1943. Out of this rather makeshift experience was born NSGr 9, which was equipped exclusively with Ju 87Ds.

In addition to this Italy-based group, Ju 87s served with eight other *Nachtschlachtgruppen*, divided among the various *Luftflotten*. In the west, night-flying Stukas operated in support of the German Ardennes offensive of December 1944. The Stukas worked in pairs, one aircraft acting as a flare-dropping 'illuminator' and the other as the attack aircraft. Fourteen of these nocturnal Ju 87s were destroyed by RAF Mosquito night fighters between September 1944 and April 1945, and others fell victim to Northrop P-61 Black Widows of the USAAF.

Stuka achievements

The day of the Junkers Ju 87 Stuka was over. If there is to be a fitting epitaph for this formidable combat aircraft, perhaps it is best summarized in modern words: the words of the US Army's Air Land Battle Doctrine.

"The best results are obtained when powerful blows are struck against critical units or areas whose loss will degrade the coherence of enemy operations in depth, and thus most rapidly accomplish the mission. From the enemy's point of view, these operations must be rapid, unpredictable, violent and disorientating. The pace must be fast enough to prevent him from taking offensive actions."

This, precisely, is what the Stuka achieved as it supported the *Wehrmacht*'s rampage across Europe in the early years of World War 2.

Stukas in the snow: German armourers unloading bombs in the Russian winter. (*via Phil Jarrett*)

Ju 87D-5s of the Royal Bulgarian Air Force, whose Stukas were used mainly against partisans in the mountainous regions of the country in the summer of 1944. Bulgaria changed sides in September 1944. (*via Phil Jarrett*)

4. Stuka Men:
Engineers and Aces

The son of a textile manufacturer, Hugo Junkers was born in Rheydt on 3 February 1859. From 1873 he studied at technical high schools in Charlottenburg, Karlsruhe and Aachen, after which he worked for various engineering concerns until 1888, when he joined the Continental Gas Company in Dessau. Together with its proprietor, Wilhelm von Oechelhauser, Junkers set up a subsidiary company to produce gas-powered engines, and in 1895 he set up his own company, Junkers & Co, for the production of gas appliances.

The enterprise does not appear to have been successful, because from 1897 to 1912 his main occupation was as a lecturer in engineering and thermodynamics at Aachen Technical High School. During his time there, he established a research laboratory to investigate the development of oil engines, a path that led him inexorably towards aircraft construction.

In 1910, Junkers patented a design for an all-metal aerofoil section for aircraft, which led to the development of the Junkers J.1 all-metal cantilever monoplane of 1915 and the establishment, on 20 October 1917, of the Junkers-Fokker-Werke AG, in collaboration with the celebrated fighter aircraft constructor Anthony Fokker. A number of successful all-metal aircraft were produced during World War I, including the J.4 ground attack aircraft and the J.9 and J.10 fighters.

In 1919, Article 201 of the Treaty of Versailles imposed a six-month restriction on the production of military aircraft and aero-engines in Germany, but in fact it was 1922 before the

Professor Hugo Junkers

restriction was lifted by the Allies. In the meantime, Junkers set up production facilities in Sweden and Russia. The company was reformed as the Junkers Flugzeugwerke AG in Dessau, and in June 1919 it produced its first all-metal commercial design, the J.13 (later F.13), one of the world's most successful transport aircraft.

The following years saw the production of types such as the single-engined W.33, which in 1928 made the first east-west Atlantic crossing by a heavier-than-air craft, and multi-engined aircraft like the G.24, G.31, G.38 and the famous Ju 52/3m airliner.

In 1933 the National Socialists came to power in Germany, and all assets and patents of the Junkers company were taken over by the State. Disillusioned, and beset by disputes with his workforce caused by the downturn in business as a result of the world depression, Junkers severed his connections with the company, which continued to produce aircraft under his name, and busied himself with private research until his death at Gauting, near Munich, on 3 February 1935.

Dipl-Ing Hermann Pohlmann

Although most Junkers designs of the 1920s were the work of Ernst Zindel and Otto Mader, Hermann Pohlmann was responsible for the design of the famous W.33/W.34 series, and played an active part in the development of other Junkers civil types. In 1928 he was involved in the development of the Junkers K.47, progenitor of the Ju 87 Stuka, which was also Pohlmann's creation.

Born on 26 June 1894, Pohlmann served in the Imperial German Air Service during World War I, being shot down, wounded and taken prisoner by the British on the Italian Front in December 1917. He joined the Junkers Flugzeugwerke in 1923 and remained with the firm until 1940, when he went to Blohm & Voss. After World War 2 he went to Spain, where he joined Spanish aircraft manufacturer CASA in 1950. Returning to Germany in 1959, he became technical director of the Hamburger Flugzeugbau GmbH (formerly Blohm & Voss). He retired in 1968.

Kurt Erfurth

Born in June 1898, Kurt Erfurth joined the Junkers company at Dessau in 1913, and from 1926 onwards he was mainly concerned with aero-engine designs, being responsible for the development of the Junkers Jumo 210, 211 (which powered the Ju 87) and 213. In May 1942 he was appointed Chief Engineer at the Junkers Motorenwerke. Captured by US troops in 1945, he went to the USA and like many of Germany's wartime engineers worked at the Aeronautical Research Laboratories, Dayton, Ohio. He retired in 1965.

Willy Neuenhofen

Willy Neuenhofen joined Junkers in 1921 and became the company's leading test pilot. On 26 May 1929 he set up a new altitude record of 12,739 m (38,854 ft), which he reached in a Junkers W.34be after a 45-minute climb. Neuenhofen was responsible for flight testing the Junkers Ju 60 and the prototype Ju 87, which flew for the first time on 17 September 1935. On 24 January 1936 he was killed during a test flight of the Ju 87V-2, which crashed due to structural failure of the tail unit.

THE ACES

Oberstleutnant Hans-Ulrich Rudel

The vast, rolling plains of Russia made excellent tank country, and nowhere else in World War 2 was armour used on such a vast scale. It followed that the use of anti-tank aircraft became of paramount importance on both sides, and in the German camp one man became the tank-hunter supreme. He was Hans-Ulrich Rudel.

Silesian-born Rudel, whose combat career was spent entirely on the Eastern Front, joined the *Luftwaffe* in 1936 and trained as a bomber pilot, although he spent most of the next three years as an observer. In 1941 he was posted to I/StG 2 Immelmann, which was equipped with Ju 87Bs, and flew his first operational sorties on 22 June, the opening day of the German offensive in Russia.

On 23 September, during an attack on the Soviet Baltic Fleet in Kronshtadt, a 1000kg (2204lb) bomb dropped by Rudel blew the bows off the battleship *Marat*, which settled on the bottom. In subsequent attacks he sank a cruiser and a destroyer. On 6 January 1942, after he had completed more than 400 operational missions, he was awarded the Knight's Cross.

After a break from operational flying Rudel was appointed *Staffelkapitan* of 9./StG 2, which had now moved to the Caucasus. He flew his 500th mission in September 1942, and reached the 1000 mark on 10 February 1943. On 1 April he was promoted to the rank of *Hauptmann*, and it was at this time, when StG 2 began to receive the cannon-armed Ju 87G, which Rudel had tested at Rechlin during his absence from the front, that his tank-busting career really began. Apart from destroying tanks, Rudel also found the Ju 87G highly effective against amphibious craft; he destroyed 70 during the battle for the Kuban bridgehead alone. On 14 April he was awarded the Oak Leaves to the Knight's Cross.

On the opening day of the Battle of Kursk, which began on 5 July 1943, Rudel quickly destroyed four Russian T-34 tanks, and by the end of the day his score had risen to twelve. In September he was appointed to command III/StG 2, and at the end of the following month he destroyed his 100th Russian tank. The award of the Swords to the Knight's Cross followed on 25 November, and promotion to *Major* on 1 March 1944.

On 26 March Rudel destroyed seventeen enemy tanks, bringing his score to 202, and after he had destroyed his 301st tank, during his 2000th sortie on 1 June, 1944, he was awarded the Diamonds to the Knight's Cross, the Pilot's Medal in Gold and the Mission Clasp in Gold and Diamonds. On 19 August 1944 Rudel was shot down and wounded, but he remained on operations and was appointed to the command of StG 2 with the rank of *Oberstleutnant*. On 29 December, 1944, Adolf Hitler presented him with a unique and specially created award, the Golden Oakleaves.

In February 1945 Rudel flew his 2400th mission, and his tally of enemy tanks destroyed had reached 505. On 8 February he was shot down by flak near Lebus, and his right foot had to be amputated. Despite this injury, he continued to fly with an artificial limb, his wound only partially healed, and destroyed 26 more tanks.

At the war's end Rudel surrendered his *Geschwader* to the Americans. Afterwards, he joined former members of the Focke-Wulf company in Argentina. He later returned to Austria, where he settled in Kufstein and worked as a ski instructor. He died in December 1982, aged 66.

Oberst Helmut Bruck

Helmut Bruck was born on 15 February 1913. After completing his schooling, Bruck became a policeman before joining the new *Luftwaffe* in 1935. On completion of his training he was

Oberstleutnant Hans-Ulrich Rudel

posted to *Gruppe* I/165, and in May 1939 he was appointed commander of No 1 *Staffel* of StG 77. In August 1940, after taking part in the Polish and French campaigns and the Battle of Britain, he became commander of I *Gruppe*, which he led in the Balkans campaign of April 1941. He was awarded the Knight's Cross in September 1941. Several times, during the campaign in Russia, he landed his aircraft behind enemy lines to rescue shot-down airmen. On 19 February 1943 he was awarded the Oak Leaves, and the next day he was given command of StG 77. In November 1943 he was promoted *Oberstleutnant*, and on 10 January 1944 he flew his 800th combat mission. He was promoted *Oberst* in June 1944 and continued to lead StG 77 until January 1945, when he assumed command of *Schulgeschwader* 151. After the war, Helmut Bruck became a forester.

Generalleutnant Walter Hagen

Generalmajor Walter Enneccerus

The man who was to become one of the *Luftwaffe*'s leading Stuka virtuosos was born on 21 November 1911. Joining the *Luftwaffe* in 1935, he served initially with I/StGr 165 before being promoted *Hauptmann* and given command of II/StG 2 in December 1939. Enneccerus fought in the Belgian and French campaigns of 1940 and in the Battle of Britain, after which II/StG 2 deployed to Trapani, Sicily, in December for operations against Malta and the British Mediterranean Fleet.

On 10 January, 1941, I/StG 1 (Paul-Werner Hozzel) and Enneccerus's II/StG 2 joined forces to inflict substantial damage on the aircraft carrier HMS *Illustrious* and light damage on the battleship HMS *Warspite*. On the following day II/StG 2 damaged the cruiser HMS *Southampton* so badly that she had to be abandoned. Enneccerus subsequently led his Stukas in North Africa, taking part in the assault on Tobruk. In April 1942 he served on the staff of *Fliegerführer Afrika*, and took part in further attacks on Malta before being appointed to command StG 77 in October. He continued in command of the *Geschwader* until February

1943, when he handed over to Helmut Bruck. Enneccerus later served on the staffs of *Fliegerführer West* and *Luftflotte* 6. In 1956 he joined the Federal German *Luftwaffe*, retiring as a *Generalmajor* in 1967. He died at Troisdorf on 3 August 1971, after a long illness.

Major Peter Gasmann

Peter Gasmann was commissioned from the ranks in the pre-war *Luftwaffe*. On 5 April 1941 he took command of III/StG 1, and in May 1942, after destroying 24 tanks, 39 artillery pieces and nine bridges, he was awarded the Knight's Cross. On 1 May 1944, as a *Major*, he assumed command of *Schlachtgeschwader* 1. Peter Gasmann was born on 4 December 1910, and died in Bonn on 6 September 1965.

Generalleutnant Walter Hagen

Born on 16 March 1897, Walter Hagen served in a Hussar regiment from 1915 to 1917, when he transferred to the Naval Air Service. After WWI he worked as a salesman for a time, then joined Junkers as a pilot in 1924. In 1930 he made the first catapult launch from a German ship. Five years later he joined the new *Luftwaffe* and worked at the Air Ministry until 1938, when he was promoted *Major* and given command of *Flugzeugtragergruppe* I/186, which was intended to operate Ju 87s from the carrier *Graf Zeppelin*. He saw action with the group in Poland.

On 18 November 1939 he was appointed commander of *Stukageschwader* 1, which he led in the battle of France, and continued in command until 30 March 1943, when he handed over to *Oberstleutnant* Gustav Pressler. Hagen was appointed *Fliegerführer* 3 with the 1st German-Italian Tank Army in the Balkans, and commanded all *Luftwaffe* formations in eastern Serbia. At the end of the war he was a *Generalleutnant* in command of the 17th *Fliegerdivision*.

Walter Hagen was awarded the Knight's Cross on 21 July 1940 and the Oak Leaves on 17 February 1942. He died in Kiel, his home town, on 24 March 1963, after a long illness.

Hauptmann Paul-Werner Hozzel

Born in Hamburg on 16 October 1910, Paul-Werner Hozzel served as an artillery officer before transferring to the *Luftwaffe* in 1935. In

Ju 87B-1s over the English Channel in the early phase of the Battle of Britain, July 1940. (*via Phil Jarrett*)

June 1939 he assumed command of I/StG 1, and on 8 May 1940 he became the first Stuka pilot to be awarded the Knight's Cross in recognition of the group's anti-shipping activities. He led the group in the Battle of Britain, the Balkans, Crete and the Mediterranean theatre, relinquishing command in May 1941. In October that year he was given command of StG 2 in Russia, and promoted to *Oberstleutnant*. In February 1943 he took command of operational elements of StGs 1, 2 and 77, which he formed into the *Gefechtsverband* (Fighting Unit) Hozzel, which was used to support German counter-attacks against Soviet forces. For these operations, Hozzel was awarded the Oak Leaves in April 1943.

Imprisoned by the Russians at the end of the war, Paul-Werner Hozzel returned to Germany in 1956 and joined the *Bundeswehr*, rising to the rank of *Brigadegeneral*. He retired to his birthplace, Hamburg, in 1971.

Hauptmann Friedrich Lang

Friedrich Lang was born on 12 January 1915. He studied physics and mathematics at university, and then aircraft construction at Breslau Technical High School. In 1935 he

Hauptmann Friedrich Lang

A *Kette* (chain of three aircraft, or flight) of Ju 87B-1s pictured over France in 1940. (*via Phil Jarrett*)

joined the infantry and then, having learned to fly privately in the meantime, he transferred to the *Luftwaffe*, eventually being accepted for flying training after being turned down several times. In January 1938 he was commissioned as a *Leutnant*, and served as an air observer on various types until July, when he was posted to *Stukagruppe* 163, when he began training on the Ju 87A and the Hs 123.

In 1939 his *Gruppe* was redesignated I/StG 2. He saw action in Poland, Belgium, Holland and France, flying his personal Stuka coded T6+HH, but on 8 June 1940, during an attack on England, he was badly wounded and hospitalized until the end of August. Lang subsequently saw action in Greece and Crete before taking part in the Russian campaign, being awarded the Knight's Cross of the Iron Cross in November 1941.

He reached the 600-mission total in August 1942, during the drive to Stalingrad, and received the Oak Leaves in November. At this time he was liaison officer at HQ *Luftflotte* 4. He returned to flying duties in March 1943 as commander of III/StG 1, which began rearming with the Focke-Wulf Fw 190 in September.

On 7 March 1944 Lang flew his 1000th operational mission, a patrol over Vitebsk. In June he was rested, taking command of *Schlachtfliegerschule* 101 at Wirschau, and in July he was awarded the Swords to the Knight's Cross. In February 1945 Lang took command of *Schlachtgeschwader* 2 from Hans-Ulrich Rudel, who had been wounded.

After the war Lang worked as a teacher, then as a building engineer, before joining the *Bundeswehr* in 1956. He served until 1967, retiring as an *Oberst*.

Oberstleutnant Gustav Pressler

At the outbreak of World War 2 Gustav Pressler was an *Oberleutnant* and *Staffelkapitan* in IV/StG 77, with whom he fought in the Polish and French campaigns. In October 1941, as a *Hauptmann*, he was given command of II/StG 2, with which he experienced heavy fighting on the Eastern Front. On 4 February 1941 Pressler was awarded the Knight's Cross, and in January 1943, after completing 500 operational missions, he received the Oak Leaves. On 1 April 1943 he took over command of StG 1, which was then rearming with Focke-Wulf Fw 190s, from Walter Hagen. In November 1944, after serving briefly on the German Military Mission in Sofia, Bulgaria, he assumed command of *Schlachtgeschwader* 104, which he led until the end of the war.

Gustav Pressler joined the *Bundeswehr* in 1956, serving until 1965.

Generalfeldmarschall Wolfram von Richthofen

A cousin of World War I 'ace of aces' Manfred von Richthofen, Wolfram von Richthofen was born on 11 October 1895 in Barzdorf, Silesia. Serving initially with a Hussar regiment in WW1, he saw action on both Eastern and Western Fronts before transferring to the Air Service. On 4 April 1918 he joined *Jasta* 11, his cousin's famous 'flying circus'. Shortly afterwards Manfred was killed. Wolfram ended the war with eight victories and was awarded the Iron Cross, 1st and 2nd class. After the war he studied engineering until 1925, when he joined the *Reichswehr*. From 1929 to 1933 he was Military Attaché in Rome, after which he transferred to the *Luftwaffe*. During the Spanish Civil War, as a *Generalmajor*, he commanded the Condor Legion, and in 1939, by now a *Generalleutnant*, he was given command of VIII

Ju 87Ds of 7./StG 1, with shirt-sleeved crews in position, preparing to take off on a sortie from their airfield near the Dniepr river in the summer of 1942. (*via Phil Jarrett*)

Junkers Ju 87Ds in flight over the USSR in 1942. The Stuka played a major part in early German successes on the Eastern Front. (via Phil Jarrett)

Fliegerkorps, whose Stuka operations he directed in all subsequent campaigns until July 1942, when he was appointed to the command of *Luftflotte* 4. A year later he was promoted *Generalfeldmarschall* and given command of *Luftflotte* 2 in the Mediterranean theatre, but in November 1944 he contracted a brain tumour and was transferred to the reserve. He died on 12 June 1945, while in captivity in an American PoW camp at Bad Ischl, Austria.

Oberst Gunter Schwarzkopff

Gunter Schwarzkopff was born on 5 August 1898 and served in the infantry during World War I. After being badly wounded at Verdun he transferred to the Air Service. He joined the *Reichswehr* after the armistice, and in 1933 served as a *Hauptmann* in the Air Ministry, where he became involved in the development of the Stuka. Schwarzkopff flew with the Condor Legion in Spain and subsequently supervised the formation of the first Stuka units. Attached to Junkers, he led the Ju 87 evaluation programme, and in 1939 he was appointed the first commander of StG 77. In May 1940, now an *Oberst*, he led the dive-bombing attacks on French positions on the Meuse. On the 14th, the day the river was crossed, he was shot down and killed, being posthumously awarded the Knight's Cross in November.

Hauptmann Johann Zemsky

Born in 1909, Johann Zemsky rose through the ranks in the artillery and was commissioned in 1936, transferring to the *Luftwaffe* two years later. During the first year of World War 2 he served as an instructor at the Insterburg *Stukaschule*, before being promoted to *Hauptmann* and given command of II/StG 1 in September 1940.

In February 1940, after completing 300 missions, he was awarded the Knight's Cross, and in July 1942, over Stalingrad, his mission total reached 500. He was shot down and killed on 28 August 1942, in the course of his 601st mission, and was posthumously awarded the Oak Leaves.

5. Stuka in service: Variants, In Flight and Users

Following the loss of the first prototype Ju 87V-1 on 24 January, 1936, subsequent development aircraft and the production Ju 87A featured a revised tail with a single fin, but the heavy 'trousers' on the fixed undercarriage of the prototype were retained, making it easy to distinguish this version from later models of the Ju 87. The 'A' model also featured two prominent radio antennae, angled outwards in a 'V' configuration from the cockpit canopy; these were later replaced by a single vertical antenna. Radio equipment was the FuG VII, which enabled the observer to transmit and receive w/t (wireless telegraphy) messages. The radiator intake was small and rectangular; this was enlarged on later models. Another difference between the Ju 87A and subsequent variants was that the A model had hinged cockpit panels instead of sliding ones.

The Ju 87A-0 pre-production model entered service in the spring of 1937. The production Ju 87A-1 was powered by the 680-hp Junkers Jumo 210D 12-cylinder inverted-vee type, driving a three-blade, two-position Jumo Hamilton propeller. The aircraft was armed with two 7.92-mm machine guns: one fixed forward-firing Rheinmetall-Borsig MG 17 in the port wing, and an MG 15 on a flexible mount in the rear cockpit, operated by the observer/gunner. Offensive load was one 458-kg (1012-lb) bomb under the fuselage with the aircraft flown solo, or a 250-kg (551-lb) bomb with two crew members. The bomb was mounted on a cradle which swung forward and downward at the moment of release, so that the bomb cleared the propeller arc. There were also two small racks for SC50 bombs under each outboard wing panel. The Ju 87 was equipped with an ingenious automatic bombing system; this consisted of an Askania autopilot, which was used together with a Revi gunsight. The bomb release gear, elevator controls, and dive brakes were linked to this system.

Before attacking the pilot would set the bomb release height. The deployment of the dive brakes automatically adjusted the elevator trim tab, and put the aircraft into a dive. When the bomb release height was reached and the bombs were dropped the autopilot adjusted elevator trim tab again, so that the aircraft became tail heavy and pulled itself out of the dive. The use of the elevator was forbidden, except in case of emergency. On the pull-out, aircraft and crew were subjected to a force of about 6g.

The Ju 87A-2 was identical to the A-1 with the exception of its radio equipment fit. Improvements included the fitting of an Ei V intercom system between the two cockpits, speech transmission facilities for the pilot, and speech and w/t facilities for the observer.

Ju 87B-1

By the outbreak of World War 2, first-line Stuka units had standardized on the Ju 87B-1, which was fitted with the more powerful 1100-hp Junkers Jumo 211A 12-cylinder engine with fuel injection, an important asset in an aircraft habitually subjected to very high g loadings. A new engine cowling was designed, with a new

Junkers Ju 87A-1 'Anton'
1./StG 162
1937

Junkers Ju 87B-1
Grupo 29, Fuerzas Aereas Nacionales
(Kampfgruppe 88, Legion Condor)
1938-39

Junkers Ju 87B-1 'Berta'
Pre-war livery, ready for delivery to an
operational unit
Deassau, 1938

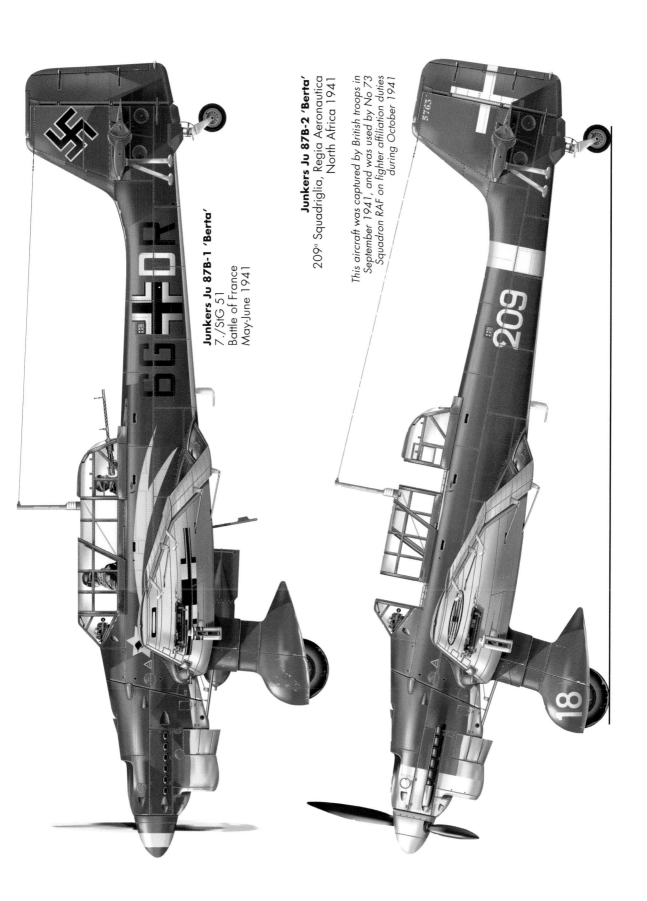

Junkers Ju 87B-1 'Berta'
7./StG 51
Battle of France
May-June 1941

Junkers Ju 87B-2 'Berta'
209ᵃ Squadriglia, Regia Aeronautica
North Africa 1941

*This aircraft was captured by British troops in
September 1941, and was used by No 73
Squadron RAF on fighter affiliation duties
during October 1941*

A Ju 87A, named Irene, picketed in the snow. Note the twin radio aerials. (*via Phil Jarrett*)

air intake on top of the cowling, and a deep half-circular radiator under it. The most obvious external change was the replacement of the A model's 'trousered' undercarriage by a 'spatted' one, with close-fitting streamlined oleo covers and streamlined wheel spats. The latter could be removed if the aircraft was required to operate from airfields covered in mud or slush. The undercarriage was slightly repositioned and strengthened, to reduce the chances of its being ripped off during operations out of rough terrain.

A less obvious modification was one which was nevertheless to endow the Stuka with a fearsome reputation: each undercarriage leg was provided with a mounting for a siren, a so-called 'Jericho Trumpet', which produced the Stuka's characteristic diving screech. This was a psychological weapon, which had a significant adverse effect on enemy morale as the dive bombers supported Germany's early conquests. The Ju 87B-1's armament was increased, an electro-pneumatic-operated Rheinmetall-Borsig 7.92mm machine gun being installed in each wing. The rear-mounted MG 15 remained unchanged.

The more powerful engine enabled the Ju 87B-1 to carry an offensive load of up to 1000 kg (2204 lb).

Ju 87B-2

Powered by a 1200-hp Junkers Jumo 211D engine with moveable radiator flaps, the B-2 model was fitted with a three-blade Junkers VS 5 or VS 11 propeller. It could be fitted with the FuG 25 IFF (Identification Friend/Foe) and Peil G IV direction finding equipment.

Ju 87C

Shipboard development of the Ju 87B, intended to form part of the planned aircraft carrier *Graf Zeppelin*'s air group. The Ju 87C's wings, which folded outboard of the undercarriage attachment points to lie flat against the fuselage sides, were of slightly smaller span that the B model. It was also fitted with an arrester hook. The undercarriage could be jettisoned in the event of a ditching, and flotation bags were provided. The Ju 87C could carry long-range underwing tanks, a feature retained on the land-based Ju 87R. The *Graf Zeppelin* was never completed, and the unit designated to operate from it, 4.(Stuka)/186, operated in Poland and France with Ju 87Bs and a few Ju 87C-0s.

Ju 87R-1

The Ju 87R-1 (the 'R' denoting *Reichweite*, or 'range'), was identical to the B-1 apart from a

An early production Ju 87B-1 in pre-war *Luftwaffe* livery. (*via Phil Jarrett*)

A three-plane *kette* of Junkers Ju 87B-1s in flight. (*via Phil Jarrett*)

revised fuel transfer system, the installation of an extra 150-litre (33 Imp gal) fuel tank in each wing and hardpoints for the carriage of two 300-litre (66 Imp gal) drop tanks under the wings. This gave the aircraft a range of 1412 km (876 miles), compared with the 550 km (342 miles) of the B-1.

Ju 87R-2 (trop)
This was an R-1 field modified with tropical

equipment for Mediterranean operations.

Ju 87R-4
Identical to the R-2 (trop) but with modifications incorporated on the assembly line. Fitted with a modified internal lubrication system, desert sand filter etc.

Ju 87D-1
During the spring of 1940, an extensive

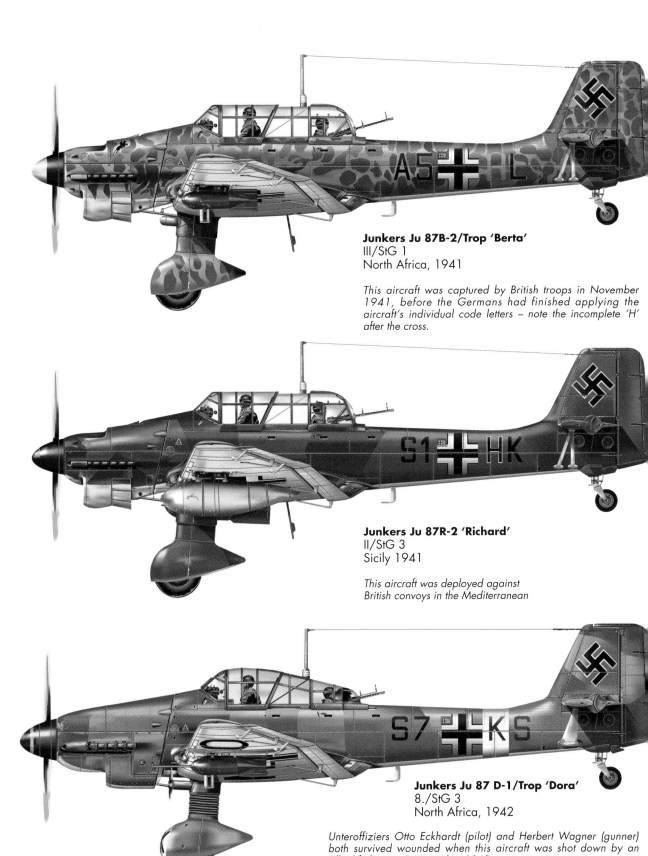

Junkers Ju 87B-2/Trop 'Berta'
III/StG 1
North Africa, 1941

This aircraft was captured by British troops in November 1941, before the Germans had finished applying the aircraft's individual code letters – note the incomplete 'H' after the cross.

Junkers Ju 87R-2 'Richard'
II/StG 3
Sicily 1941

This aircraft was deployed against British convoys in the Mediterranean

Junkers Ju 87 D-1/Trop 'Dora'
8./StG 3
North Africa, 1942

Unteroffiziers Otto Eckhardt (pilot) and Herbert Wagner (gunner) both survived wounded when this aircraft was shot down by an Allied fighter on 1 November 1942

Junkers Ju 87D-1/Trop 'Dora'
Oberstleutnant Walter Sigel
Commander, StG 3
North Africa 1942

Junkers Ju 87D-3 'Dora'
4./StG 2
Stalingrad
September 1942/February 1943

Junkers Ju 87D-3 'Dora'
Grupul 6 Bombardement Picaj
Royal Romanian Air Force
Eastern Front
1943

Junkers Ju 87Ds in flight. The reprofiled nose and more streamlined canopy of the 'D' model make it easy to distinguish from earlier variants of the Stuka. (*via Phil Jarrett*)

redesign of the basic Ju 87 airframe was undertaken to accommodate the new 1400-hp Junkers Jumo 211J engine.

Designated Ju 87D, the new variant was given more refined nose contours, achieved by re-positioning the oil cooler below the engine from its previous position above it, and also moving the oil coolant radiator to a new position below the wing, inboard of the undercarriage legs. The aircraft was fitted with a VS 11 propeller with paddle blades. The cockpit canopy was reconstructed, being tapered towards the rear, and fuel tankage was similar to that of the Ju 87R. The variant was fitted with an undercarriage jettison facility, as in the C model, and the wheeled undercarriage could be replaced by skis.

The defensive armour was upgraded, and the single 7.92-mm machine gun in the rear cockpit was replaced by a twin MG 81Z of similar calibre. The bomb load was also substantially increased, provision being made for a 1800-kg (4000-lb) bomb under the fuselage and either four 50-kg (110-lb) or two 500-kg (1102-lb) bombs under the wings. In practice the 1800-kg bomb was rarely carried, most

aircraft being armed with a 1400-kg (3085-lb) armour-piercing bomb or a 1000-kg (2204-lb) general purpose weapon.

The aircraft could carry a WB 81 or WB FF container under each wing, the former accommodating six MG 81 machine guns and the latter two 20-mm MG FF cannon. The prototype D-1 (Ju 87V-21) flew for the first time in February 1941. The first productiion models were the D-1 and D-1 (trop).

Ju 87D-2

This variant was identical to the D-1, but was fitted with a strengthened tailwheel and a glider towing hook combination.

Ju 87D-3

Identical to the D-2, but with the sirens deleted and their housings faired over. The fuselage undersides and coolant lines were armoured to give extra protection against ground fire.

Ju 87D-4

Similar to the D-3, but intended for anti-ship operations with provision for carrying a torpedo. Not proceeded with.

A Ju 87D-1 (Trop) with 66 Imp gal underwing fuel tanks. Note the large paddle-blade propeller. (*via Phil Jarrett*)

This Junkers Ju 87D-3 was an experimental passenger-carrying variant. It was fitted with wing-mounted personnel pods and tested at the Graf Zeppelin Research Institute at Ruit, near Stuttgart, in 1944. The pods, designed to carry two men each, were non-jettisonable. (*via Phil Jarrett*)

Junkers Ju 87D-5 'Dora'
2 Pulk Szturmovy
Royal Bulgarian Air Force
Anti-partisan operations
Summer 1944

Junkers Ju 87D-5 'Dora'
Grupul 3 Bombardement Picaj
Forele Aeriene Regale ale Romaniei
(Royal Romanian Air Force)
Crimean Peninsula
Late 1943

Junkers Ju 87D-5 'Dora'
1./SG 2 'Immelmann'
Russian Front
Winter 1943-1944

Junkers Ju 87G-1 'Gustav Production Prototype'
Tank Combat Experimental Unit
Russian Front
March 1943

Junkers Ju 87D-8 'Dora'
1. Staffel
Night Attack Gruppe 1
Western Europe
Winter 1944-1945

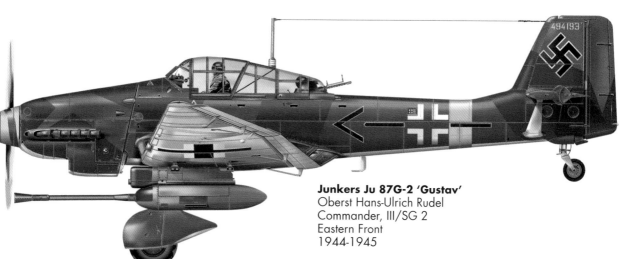

Junkers Ju 87G-2 'Gustav'
Oberst Hans-Ulrich Rudel
Commander, III/SG 2
Eastern Front
1944-1945

The drag of the cannon pods carried by the Ju 87G tank destroyer made it very slow, but it was a very accurate weapons platform in the hands of a skilled pilot. (*via Phil Jarrett*)

Ju 87D-5

Similar to the D-3, but with wing span increased to 15.0 m (45 ft 3.5 in). Wing-mounted machine guns replaced by 20-mm Mauser MG 151 cannon. The combined bomb release and automatic pull-out system was divided into a dual system, each component controlled by a push button for trim compensation and bomb release.

Ju 87D-6

Similar to the D-5.

Ju 87D-7

Night ground attack variant, fitted with a 1500-hp Junkers Jumo 211P engine with flame dampers over the engine exhaust stubs.

Ju 87D-8

Similar to Ju 87D-7.

Ju 87E

Projected navalised version of the Ju 87D; not built.

Ju 87F

Projected improved version of the Ju 87D, with a fully retractable undercarriage, a 1776-hp Jumo 213A engine, two forward-firing MG 151 20-mm cannon, and a dorsal barbette housing an MG 151 cannon and an MG 131 machine gun. Project abandoned; also given the RLM designation Ju 187.

Ju 87G-1

Specialist tank destroyer, based on a rebuilt D-3 airframe and armed with two 37-mm Flak 18 cannon slung under the wings outboard of each main undercarriage leg. Some G-1s had the muzzles of the wing-mounted MG 17s faired over. Bomb racks, dive brakes, oxygen system and other non-essential systems eliminated to save weight.

Ju 87G-2

As G-1, but based on rebuilt D-5 airframe. Original fixed armament removed, resulting in clean wing leading edge.

Ju 87H

The Ju 87H models (H-1, H-3, H-5, H-7 and H-8) were unarmed versions of the equivalent D-models, equipped with dual controls, for use as trainers. The rear cockpit design was again modified, with bulged window panels to give the instructor a reasonable view forward. A

The Ju 87H was an unarmed trainer version of the Stuka, in which the gunner's position was replaced by a second forward-facing pilot's seat, the latter taken from an Arado Ar 96 trainer. The aircraft had a bulged rear cockpit for improved forward vision. (*via Phil Jarrett*)

forward-facing Ar 96 seat was installed. The aircraft could be fitted with a ski undercarriage.

Ju 87K

The Ju 87K designation was used for export models. The K-1 was equivalent to the A-1 and intended for export to Japan. The K-2 and K-4, equivalent to the B-1 and A-1, were exported to Hungary.

In flight

Operating the Ju 87 (with the exception of the Ju 87G variant, whose twin cannon made it unstable) was straightforward enough. The pilot first of all switched the fuel cock to the 'both tanks' position, gave a few strokes of the primer, switched on the fuel booster pumps, set the throttle to the figure '1' on the quadrant, switched on both magnetos and energised the

inertia starter and booster coil by pushing in a handle on the lower left side for ten seconds, then pulling out the handle until the engine fired. The engine could be run up to 1600 rpm on the brakes, or 2200 rpm with the tail tied down to prevent the Stuka from nosing over. Taxiing could be tricky, as the aircraft required a good deal of braking to manoeuvre and was sensitive to any crosswind.

Take-off

Once the take-off position had been reached the pilot taxied the aircraft forward for a short distance to straighten the tailwheel, which was then locked. The drill then was to switch on the fuel pumps, set the flaps to the take-off position, the trim tabs to zero and the propeller pitch lever to START. Acceleration was good, the Stuka becoming airborne after a run of

There was little aesthetic appeal about the Ju 87, which was a very large aircraft for a single engine to support. But it was instantly identifiable, and the sight of its crank-winged form about to nose over into a dive was enough to inspire terror in the early years of the war. (*via Phil Jarrett*)

about 457 m (500 yards) at a speed of 116 km/h (72 mph). Initial climb was at 215 km/h (133 mph), the supercharger being moved from low gear to the automatic position at 3500 m (11,480 ft). The climb was laborious, the aircraft taking some 20 minutes to reach 5000 m (16,400 ft)

Diving

Before entering a dive, the Stuka pilot went through the following check list:

Landing flaps at cruise position
Elevator trim at cruise position
Rudder trim at cruise position
Propeller pitch set at cruise
Contact altimeter - ON
Contact altimeter set to release altitude
Supercharger set at automatic
Throttle fully closed

Cooler flaps closed
Dive brakes open

The action of opening the dive brakes made the Stuka nose over under the influence of the pull-out mechanism, which was itself activated by opening the dive brakes. To enable the pilot to judge the dive angle accurately – not an easy thing to do without some form of artifical aid – a series of graduations was etched on the front starboard side of the cockpit canopy.

Speed in the dive built up rapidly to 540 km/h (335mph) in about 1370 m (4500 ft), increasing relatively slowly to a maximum permissible speed of 600km/h (373 mph). As the Stuka dived, the pilot kept an eye on a warning light on the contact altimeter; when this illuminated, he pressed a knob on the control column, activating the automatic pull-

Landing the Stuka was straightforward but required the pilot's full attention, as the aircraft had a tendency to nose over on touchdown. (*via Phil Jarrett*)

out. The aircraft required 450 m (1475 ft) to recover to level flight, being subjected to a force of 6g in the process. The pilot could override the automatic pull-out and complete the operation manually, although this required considerable strength and careful use of the elevator trimmer. As the nose came up through the horizon the dive brakes were retracted, the propeller pitch set to take-off/climb, and the throttle and radiator flaps opened.

Landing

Landing was straightforward, speed being reduced to about 200 km/h (125mph) on the downwind leg of the aerodrome circuit and 180 km/h (112mph) on the crosswind leg. The tailwheel was locked, propeller pitch set to fully fine, and final approach made at 150 km/h (93mph), reducing to 120 km/h (75 mph) at the flare-out. Thanks to the pilot's raised

position, the view on the approach and landing was excellent. A three-point landing was desirable, as the Stuka had a tendency to nose over. There was an inherent weakness in the undercarriage design that could lead to failure of the upper mainwheel fork and subsequent collapse of the wheel assembly.

Many Allied pilots had the opportunity to fly the Ju 87. One of them was Squadron Leader D.H. Clarke, a self-confessed 'type hog' who lost no chance of flying as many different aircraft as possible and who was an instructor with an operational training unit in Egypt in 1944. His recollection of the Stuka was far from favourable, although in fairness the example he flew had been much abused both before and after its capture.

"Wing Commander Mike Lyne 'phoned me from Ballah, a salt lake aerodrome alongside the Suez Canal, and said that I could have a crack at their Stuka if I wanted to, but I had better make it soon because it was due to be scrapped. I flew over from Fayid the next day to find that Mike had not exaggerated about its condition. The British camouflage was peeling, the wheel spats had been removed – as had many other bits and pieces. The perspex glasshouse was scratched and broken; RAF roundels, looking absurdly out of place, completed the picture of captured resignation. The vulture was in an advanced state of decay.

"The rumble of the Jumo 211J engine, when I started up, retained a little of its ferocity as though it could remember past victories; but the husky growl of old age can never imitate the snarl of aggression, and the fuselage rattled and shook from the rough running. The cockpit was roomy and the visibility all round was excellent – there was even a perspex panel in the floor so that the pilot could view the target between his legs. I failed to see the point of this refinement. After many dive-bombing experiences in Skuas and Kittyhawks, the only method I knew of going down was to put the target under one wing and then peel over and aim directly at it. Fancy contoured lines were painted around the inside of the windscreen and the hood and marked in degrees. Obviously they were for the pilot to line against the horizon and thereby know the angle of his dive – but what good did that do him? Usually you had enough worries trying to keep the nose pointed at the target, without bothering about judging the angle!

"I taxied out. The take-off was longer than I thought it would be, and it seemed strange not to have an undercarriage to retract. The climb was laborious. A Kittyhawk, pre-arranged, darted out of the sun and I turned to meet it, clawing for height and aiming just under its belly as I had done so many times against 109s. But the Stuka could not hold the angle, juddered, stalled, and fell into a dive. It was like flying a brick. I was shot down a dozen times that morning. My opponent was only a clapped-out P-40, so against a Spitfire or a Hurricane there would only be one answer – there only ever was one answer!

"The dive brakes were unserviceable but I tried a shallow dive without them, aiming for

the Anzac Memorial overlooking Lake Timsah. When the ASI was indicating 400 kilometers (per hour), the aircraft was disliking it so much that I pulled out cautiously – at 250 mph the controls were stiffer than a Kittyhawk at nearly double the speed. Maybe it was different with the dive brakes down, maybe rheumatics had set in, maybe... Nevertheless I was very glad that I had never had to fly them on ops! I returned to Ballah and eased the creaking carcase into a gentle landing."

Ground strafing

Although the Ju 87 could survive in a hostile environment as a dive bomber, provided it had adequate fighter cover, ground strafing was a different and much more risky enterprise, as Hungarian Stuka pilot and squadron commander Gyozo Levay found to his cost.

"My unit, the 102/1 Dive Bomber Squadron of the Royal Hungarian Air Force, was stationed at Grodek-Jagiellonski airfield, Poland, in July 1944, attached to III Gruppe of *Stukageschwader* 77. The group commander was away on leave and the leader of 7 *Staffel*, *Hauptmann* N., was deputising for him. *Hauptmann* N., a fair-haired man, was the only German squadron leader in the group who had not yet been awarded the Knight's Cross of the Iron Cross. Being in command temporarily he must have reasoned that this was the time to earn this high decoration. Each time we flew a mission and the bombs were released, he swooped down and strafed the target with machine gun fire. In the summer of 1944 this was sheer madness. The Ju 87D-5 was, by any standard, a slow and vulnerable machine, vulnerable not only to anti-aircraft guns, but also to small arms fire. It was designed for dive-bombing and not for low level attack. As a result of this selfishly displayed heroism we lost seven planes in two days...

"Reports came in that the Russians were preparing for an attack south-west of Kowel and we were to fly a sortie at once. When we reached the briefing room the Germans were already taking off. A short briefing, then the seven Hungarian Ju 87s raced along the field in close echelon formation and rose in the air.

"We reached the target area in about 85 minutes. The Hungarian squadron was the

Ju 87D-5s of the Royal Hungarian Air Force over the Eastern Front in 1944. (*via Phil Jarrett*)

second last to dive, not an enviable position. I threw my Ju 87 into an 80-degree dive. The ground rushed up rapidly and trenches, trees and enemy vehicles seemed to come at me at terrific speed. A slight correction on the rudder and the target moved into my bombsight. A slight pull on the stick – I pressed the button and the bombs were gone. But instead of pulling out sharply I flattened the dive, keeping as close to the ground as I could. I pulled the airbrakes in. As I raced low over the countryside I spotted *Hauptmann* N. and his formation, about five of them. They were waiting for the right moment to sneak in and attack.

"Normally after I had made an attack I would pull up and return to base, but this time it was to be different. Earlier, *Hauptmann* N. had inferred that I was too cowardly to return and make a strafing attack with machine guns. It was a foolhardy act, but I was determined. I banked at just under 1000 feet. As I raced back towards the target area the bombs of the last wave were exploding. I was down to fifty feet. Vehicles were now in my gunsight.

"I shoved the throttle forward... nose down still further. My finger pushed against the firing button and tracers cut through the trucks. Tree-tops raced past my cabin and panic-stricken

soldiers scattered. I pulled over in a steep bank to starboard just as a terrific explosion jarred the Ju 87. We were hit! Acrid smoke filled the cabin, the engine began to miss. A quick glance at the instrument panel, however, assured me that we could keep going for a little while, at least. Could we make the German lines?

"I called my gunner to ask if he was all right. No reply. I repeated the question. Silence. The engine was missing badly. I looked over my shoulder; Corporal Sarkady was hanging on the straps, motionless, he seemed to be dead... Now I was flying in my crippled plane, thick smoke pouring out of the engine, with a dead gunner in the rear seat. I had to concentrate on flying the violently shaking machine. In the cabin the smoke nearly blinded me. I pressed the release lever and the canopy flew off, almost taking my arm with it. At last I could see. The altimeter showed 900 feet, but the speed kept dropping back. I pushed the stick forward, the nose dropped and the needle of the airspeed indicator began to creep up.

"A large green meadow appeared in front of me and I calculated that I must have been over our side of the front, or pretty near to it, therefore I decided to land. Having a second look, somehow the meadow seemed too green to me. I remembered some good advice: if you must make a forced landing on unknown territory, no matter how smooth it looks, blow off your undercarriage, because a belly landing is better than a broken neck. I pressed the button. There was a thundering sound and the undercarriage shot past the wing trailing edges. I had never pancaked before, so I was on the alert. Gliding at 80 mph, the ground raced towards me like a huge, green carpet. I lifted the nose in three-point landing position, so that the tail would touch the ground first. The aircraft lost speed rapidly. A slight pull on the stick, the nose did not rise. So far, so good!

"Heavens, the fuel switch! As I reached forward with my left hand to switch it off, I pulled the stick lightly. A terrible impact, a splash, my old kite hit the ground skidding wildly, then finally came to a sudden halt. My head hit the instrument panel and everything went black."

Fortunately for Levay, his gunner was far from dead. Corporal Sarkady, who had suffered superficial wounds, dragged the pilot clear. The pair struggled out of the swamp in which the Stuka had landed – which accounted for the bright green colour of the grass – and were picked up by German troops. It was only then that they learned that they had walked through a minefield...

First-line Stuka Geschwader
STUKAGESCHWADER 1
Formed in the summer of 1939. Staff flight from *Stab*/LG 2, I *Gruppe* from *Sturzkampfgruppe* 160, II *Gruppe* from III/*Sturzkampfgeschwader* 41, and III *Gruppe* from *Bordfliegergruppe* 186. I *Gruppe* amalgamated with II/StG 3 on 13 January 1942. A special tank-destroyer *Staffel* (10 *Staffel*) formed in June 1943. Unit redesignated *Schlachtgeschwader* 1 in November 1943.
Operations:
Poland (1939), Denmark, Norway, Battle of Britain (1940), Malta, North Africa, Greece, Crete (1941), Soviet Union (1941-44)
Geschwader Commanders:
Oberst Walter Hagen, 10 September 1939; *Oberstleutnant* Gustav Pressler, 1 April 1943; *Major* Peter Gasmann, 1 April 1944
I Gruppe Commander:
Hauptmann Paul-Werner Hozzel, 1940-41
II Gruppe Commanders:

Hauptmann Anton Keil, 1 October 1939; *Hauptmann* Johann Zemsky, 1 September 1940; *Hauptmann* Karl Schrepfer, 1 September 1942; *Major* Ernst Reusch, 1 May 1944; *Hauptmann* Heinrich Heins, 1 February 1945
III Gruppe Commanders:
Major Walter Hagen, 1 September 1939; *Hauptmann* Helmut Mahlke, 2 July 1940; *Hauptmann* Peter Gasmann, 15 April 1942; *Hauptmann* Friedrich Lang, 1 April 1943; *Hauptmann* Karl Schrepfer, 1 May 1944
Schlachtgeschwader 1 began rearming with the Focke-Wulf Fw 190 in 1943.

STUKAGESCHWADER 2
Formed on 1 May 1939, I *Gruppe* at Cottbus, II *Gruppe* at Stolp-Reitt and III *Gruppe* at Langensalza. Staff Flight formed on 15 October 1939 at Cologne. II *Gruppe* absorbed into III/StG 3 in January 1942. Renamed *Schlachtgeschwader* 2 on 18 October 1943. Anti-tank *Staffel* (10 *Staffel*) formed June 1943.
Operations:
Poland (1939), France, Battle of Britain (1940), the Balkans, USSR, North Africa (1941), USSR, Mediterranean (1942), USSR (1943)
Geschwader Commanders:
Oberstleutnant Oskar Dinort, 15 October 1939; *Oberstleutnant* Paul-Werner Hozzel, 16 October 1941; *Oberstleutnant* Ernst Kupfer, 13 February 1943; *Oberleutnant* Hans-Karl Stepp, 10 September 1943
I Gruppe Commanders:
Major Oskar Dinort, 1 May 1939; *Hauptmann* Hubertus Hitschold, 1 October 1939; *Major* Bruno Dilley, 15 October 1941; *Hauptmann* Kurt Lau, 1 May 1944; *Hauptmann* Herbert Bauer, 23 November 1944
II Gruppe Commanders:
Major Walter Enneccerus, 1940; Unknown, 1941-42; *Major* Kurt Kennel, 18 October 1943
III Gruppe Commanders:
Hauptmann Heinz Brückner, 1 May 1939; *Hauptmann* Ernst-Siegfried Steen, 1 August 1941; *Hauptmann* Gustav Pressler, 1 October 1941; *Hauptmann* Walter Krauss, 1 April 1943; *Hauptmann* Hans-Ulrich Rudel, 19 July 1943; *Hauptmann* Lothar Rau, 1 August 1944; *Major* Müller, 23 January 1945
Schlachtgeschwader 2 began rearming with the Focke-Wulf Fw 190 in 1943, but continued to

A *Staffel* of Ju 87 Stukas flies in tight formation early in the war. In the absence of effective fighter opposition, such a formation could rip the heart out of enemy ground units. (*via Phil Jarrett*)

use the Ju 87G-1 in the anti-tank role.

STUKAGESCHWADER 3

Formed on 9 July 1940 from *Stab*/KG 28; I *Gruppe* formed from I/StG 76. II *Gruppe* formed on 13 January 1942 from I StG 1 and III *Gruppe* on 13 January 1942 from II/StG 2. Renamed *Schlachtgeschwader* 3 on 18 October 1943.

Operations:
Battle of Britain (1940), Romania and Greece (I *Gruppe* only, 1941); Mediterranean and North Africa, 1942; Tunisia, Yugoslavia, Greece, USSR (1943)

Geschwader Commanders:
Oberst Karl Angerstein, July 1940; *Oberstleutnant* Georg Edert, 27 July 1940; *Oberstleutnant* Karl Christ, 1 April 1941; *Oberstleutnant* Walter Siegel, 1 September 1941; *Oberst* Kurt Kuhlmey, 1 April 1943

I Gruppe Commanders:

Major Walter Siegel, 9 July 1940; *Hauptmann* Heinrich Eppen, April 1942; *Hauptmann* Horst Schiller, 1943

II Gruppe Commanders:
Hauptmann Paul Werner Hozzel, 1940; *Major* Sorge, 31 May 1941; *Major* Kurt Kuhlmey, 1 January 1941; *Hauptmann* Hans Neumann, 1 April 1942

III Gruppe Commanders:
Major Bernhard Hamester, 15 October 1942; *Hauptmann* Eberhard Jacob, 1 December 1943; *Hauptmann* Siegfried Goebel, May 1944; *Hauptmann* Erich Bunge, March 1945

Schlachtgeschwader 3 began rearming with the Focke-Wulf Fw 190 in 1943.

STUKAGESCHWADER 5

Formed in the summer of 1942 from IV/LG 1 with four *Staffeln*. Amalgamated with I/StG 1 in the summer of 1943, but redesignated

Ju 87Bs early in the war. At that time, Stukas like these seemed to fulfil every hope that the *Luftwaffe* high command had of the type. (*via Phil Jarrett*)

Schlachtgeschwader 5 in October that year.
Operations:
Northern Norway and Finland, 1942-45
Geschwader Commanders:
Major Hans-Karl Stepp, January 1942; *Major* Erwin Schulz, November 1942; *Major* Martin Mobus, April 1943
Non-operational after early 1944. Replaced by *Nachtschlachtgruppe* 8, also with Ju 87s.

STUKAGESCHWADER 51
Formed on 1 May 1939 with only one group (III *Gruppe*) and armed with Ju 87Bs. Absorbed into II *Gruppe* StG.1, July 1940.
Operations:
Poland, 1939
Geschwader Commander:
Major von Klitzing, May 1940-July 1941

STUKAGESCHWADER 76
Formed on 1 May 1939 (I *Gruppe* only) from I *Gruppe* StG 168. Absorbed into I/StG 3, 9 July 1940.
Operations:
Poland, 1939; France (with II *Fliegerkorps*)
Geschwader Commander:
Hauptmann Siegel, May 1939-July 1940

All too soon the Stuka's vulnerability to modern fighter opposition became obvious, and by the time this wrecked Ju 87 of StG 3 was abandoned in Tunisia in 1943, the Stuka had had its day. (*via Phil Jarrett*)

STUKAGESCHWADER 77
Formed on 1 May 1939 with I and II *Gruppe*n; III *Gruppe* formed 9 July 1940 from II/KG 76. II *Gruppe* absorbed into III *Gruppe*, *Schlachtgeschwader* 10, on 18 October 1943; remainder of StG 77 redesignated *Schlachtgeschwader* 77.
Operations:
Poland 1939, France, Battle of Britain 1940, Russia 1941-43
Geschwader Commanders:
Oberst Gunter Schwarzkopff, 1 June 1939; *Major* Graf Clemens von Schonborn-Wiesentheid, 15 May 1940; *Major* Alfons Orthofer, 25 July 1942; *Major* Walter Enneccerus, 13 October 1942; *Major* Helmut Bruck, 20 February 1943
I Gruppe Commanders:
Hauptmann Friedrich-Karl Freiherr von Dalwigk zu Lichtenfels, 1 May 1939; *Hauptmann* Meisel, 14 July 1940; *Hauptmann* Helmut Bruck, 20 August 1940; *Major* Werner Roell, 20 February 1943
II Gruppe Commanders:
Hauptmann Graf Clemens von Schonborn-Wiesentheid, 1 May 1939; *Hauptmann* Waldemar Plewig, 15 May 1940; *Major* Kurt Huhn, 1 July 1942; *Hauptmann* Helmut Leicht, 1 April 1943
III Gruppe Commanders:
Hauptmann Helmut Bode, 9 July 1940; *Hauptmann* Georg Jakob, 26 August 1942; *Hauptmann* Franz Kieslich, 1 January 1943
The Geschwader began rearming with the Focke-Wulf Fw 190 in 1943.

Appendix 1
Specifications

The Stuka and its rivals

Junkers Ju 87A-1
Type: two-seat dive bomber
Powerplant: one 680-hp Junkers Jumo 210D 12-cylinder inverted-Vee type engine
Span: 13.80 m (45 ft 3.3 in)
Length: 10.80 m (35 ft 5.25 in)
Height: 3.90 m (12 ft 9.5 in)
Maximum speed: 320 km/h (199 mph)
Service ceiling: 8000 m (26,250 ft)
Maximum range: 1000 km (621 miles)
Weights: 2300 kg (5071 lb) empty; 3400 kg (7497 lb) maximum take-off
Armament: one 7.92-mm MG 17 machine gun in fixed port wing installation; one 7.92-mm MG 15 machine gun on flexible mounting in rear cockpit; one 550-kg (1102-lb) or one 250-kg (551-lb) bomb under the fuselage, depending on whether the aircraft carried one or two crew members

Arado Ar 81V-3
Type: two-seat dive bomber
Powerplant: one 640-hp Junkers Jumo 210c water-cooled inverted-V12
Span: 11.00 m (36 ft 0.75 in)
Length: 11.50 m (37 ft 8.75 in)
Height: 3.61 m (11 ft 10 in)
Maximum speed: 314 km/h (214 mph)
Service ceiling: not known
Maximum range: 716 km (430 mph)
Weights: 1925 kg (4244 lb) empty; maximum take-off 3070 kg (6768 lb)
Armament (proposed): one forward-firing synchronized nose mounted 7.92 mm machine gun; one flexible 7.92-mm machine gun in rear cockpit; one 250-kg (551-lb) bomb

Heinkel He 118V-3
Type: two-seat dive bomber
Powerplant: one 750-hp Daimler-Benz DB600 12-cylinder Vee-type engine
Span: 15.03 m (49 ft 2.25 in)
Length: 12.16 m (39 ft 10.5 in)
Height: 3.95 m (12 ft 11.5 in)
Maximum speed: 418 km/h (260 mph)
Service ceiling: 9506 m (31,168 ft)
Maximum range: 1050 km (653 miles)
Weights: 2727 kg (6019 lb) empty; 4145 kg (9149 lb) maximum take-off
Armament (proposed): two fixed forward-firing 7.92-mm MG 17 machine guns, and one flexible 7.92-mm MG 15 machine gun in rear cockpit; either one 500-kg (1102-lb) or one 250-kg (551-lb) bomb internally

Junkers Ju 87D-5
Type: two-seat dive bomber
Powerplant: one 1,300 hp Junkers Jumo 211J 12-cylinder inverted-Vee type engine
Span: 15.25 m (50 ft 0.5 in)
Length: 11.1 m (36 ft 5 in)
Height: 3.90 m (12 ft 9.5 in)
Maximum speed: 402 km/h (250 mph)
Service ceiling: 7320 m (24,000 ft)
Maximum range: (with bomb load) 1000 km (621 miles)
Weights: 2750 kg (5071 lb) empty; 6585 kg (14,500 lb) fully loaded
Armament: two 7.92-mm MG 17 machine gun in wings; one 7.92-mm MG 81 twin-barrel machine gun on flexible mounting in rear cockpit; maximum bombload of one 1800-kg (3,968-lb) bomb on centreline

Blohm & Voss Ha 137V-5
Type: Single-seat dive bomber and assault aircraft
Powerplant: one 610-hp Junkers Jumo 210Aa water-cooled in-line engine
Span: 11.15 m (36 ft 7 in)
Length: 9.46 m (31 ft 0.75 in)
Height: 2.8 m (9 ft 2.25 in)
Maximum speed: 330 km/h (205 mph)
Service ceiling: not known
Maximum range: 580 km (360 miles)
Weights: 1814 kg (4000 lb) empty; 2415 kg (5324 lb) maximum take-off
Armament (proposed): two 7.92-mm MG 17 machine guns in upper forward fuselage and two more (or one 20-mm FF cannon) in top of landing gear 'trousers'; four 50-kg (110lb) bombs on underwing racks

Henschel Hs 123
Type: single-seat close support biplane
Powerplant: one 880-hp BMW 132Dc radial
Span: 10.50 m (34 ft 5 in)
Length: 8.33 m (27 ft 4 in)
Height: 3.20 m (10 ft 6 in)
Maximum speed: 340 km/h (211 mph)
Service ceiling: 9000 m (29,530 ft)
Maximum range: 855 km (531 miles)
Weights: 1500 kg (3307 lb) empty; 2215 kg (4884 lb) maximum take-off
Armament: two fixed forward-firing 7.92-mm MG 17 machine guns; up to 450 kg (992 lb) of bombs

Appendix 2
Weapons and Systems

Guns and Cannon

The Rheinmetall-Borsig 7.92-mm MG 15 machine gun originally carried by the Ju 87 was developed in 1934 and was designed for a flexible mounting, which made it ideal for use as a defensive weapon in aircraft. Its development was somewhat tortuous, because the Versailles treaty of 1919 had forbidden the development of any form of sustained-fire weapon in Germany. Rheinmetall-Borsig neatly sidestepped this restriction by setting up a 'shadow' factory across the border at Solothurn in Switzerland, where it developed the Solothurn Modell 1930 air-cooled machine gun. This in turn was developed into the MG 15, which remained in production for the *Luftwaffe* for many years. It had a muzzle velocity of 765 metres/sec and weighed 8.1kg.

The fixed forward-firing weapon, the MG 17, was also of 7.92 mm calibre and was developed specifically by Rheinmetall-Borsig for use in aircraft. Like the MG 15, it weighed 8.1kg, but its muzzle velocity was 905 metres/sec and it had a rate of fire of 1180 rounds per minute.

In the Ju 87D model, the defensive MG 15 was replaced by the 7.92-mm MG 81, developed by

Mauser in 1938. This was belt-fed with a rate of fire of 1060 rounds per minute and a muzzle velocity of 850 metres/sec. The MG 81Z carried by the Ju 87D had two barrels, the Z denoting *Zwilling* (twin). Cyclic rate of fire was 3000 rounds per minute.

In the Ju 87D-5 the wing-mounted MG 17s were replaced by two Mauser MG 151/20 20-mm cannon. This installation was also proposed for the Ju 87F (Ju 187), which was not proceeded with.

The heaviest gun carried by the Ju 87 series was the 37-mm Flak 18 cannon, two of which were carried by the Ju 87G in its tank-busting role. The 3-lb shells had a special tungsten core, enabling them to penetrate the top, rear or side armour of a Russian T-34 tank before exploding.

Bombs

The Ju 87A could carry a bomb of up to 500 kg (1102 lb) on its under-fuselage cradle. This was increased to 1000 kg (2204 lb) on the strengthened Ju 87B, which was also fitted with racks for small bombs under the outer wings. The Ju 87D could carry an 1800 kg (3968 lb) bomb under the fuselage, but in practice this was rarely done.

An experimental 20-mm MG 151 cannon installation in a Ju 87B. Mounted in the wing root, this weapon replaced the wing-mounted machine guns in the Ju 87D-5.

Close-up of the Flak 18 37-mm cannon fitted to the Ju 87G-1. In this photograph, the aircraft has been chocked to hold it steady while the guns are harmonized at the firing butts.

Abandoned bombs lie beside the wrecks of the Ju 87s which would have carried them. They are seen following the *Luftwaffe's* evacuation of Tunisia in 1943.

Appendix 3
Junkers Ju 87 Production

Production centres

9 prototypes built at Dessau, c/n 4921-4929
583 aircraft built at Dessau
5930 aircraft built at Weserflug Bremen, Lemwerder and Tempelhof

Annual production figures

1936	4
1937	7
1938	136
1939	577
1940	769
1941	1074
1942	1069
1943	2630
1944	1071

Foreign Ju 87 operators

Royal Hungarian Air Force:
2 Ju 87B and 1 Ju 87A delivered in 1940
4 Ju 87A in 1942
30 Ju 87D in 1943
10 Ju 87B and 18 Ju 87D in 1944

Regia Aeronautica:
58 Ju 87B delivered during 1940
42 aircraft delivered in 1941
49 Ju87D-3 transferred from *Luftwaffe* in 1943

Romanian Air Force:
54 Ju 87D aircraft delivered in 1943,
50 aircraft delivered in 1944, probably transferred from *Luftwaffe*

Czech Air Force:
Some ex-*Luftwaffe* Ju 87Ds taken over in 1945; Czech designation B37

Appendix 4
Museum Aircraft and Survivors

Although more than 6,500 Ju 87s were built between 1936 and 1944, the Junkers dive bomber led a hard life and very few survived the end of the war. In fact, there are just two complete specimens in the world's museum collections, although there are a number of incomplete or unrestored Stukas in German museums.

UNITED KINGDOM
Royal Air Force Museum, Hendon, London
Ju 87D-5 RI+JK
This aircraft was captured by British Forces in Northern Germany at the end of the war and transferred to the Royal Aircraft Establishment at Farnborough. In the sixties it was used for the film *Battle of Britain*. Special bomb equipment was integrated, while the wing cannon were removed. Since 1978 this aircraft has been displayed in the colours of 10.(Pz) *Staffel* of II/*Schlachtgeschwader* 3.

UNITED STATES
Museum of Science and Industry, Chicago
Ju 87R-2; A5+HL; s.no 5954; 1./StG 1
Captured by British Forces in Libya in 1941 and later transferred to the USA. It was displayed at the EAA Air Museum in Hales Corners before being acquired by the Museum of Science and Industry.

Ju 87R-2 0875709 IV(St)/LG 1 (later I/StG 5)
Wreck reportedly recovered in Russia in 1990 and sold to a collector in the USA.

GERMANY
Flugausstellung Leo Junior, Hermeskeil
This large private museum in the Hunsruck has some Stuka instrument panels, found in a scrapyard at Karlsruhe in the early 1980s. One panel was rebuilt and is now on display.

Auto + Technik Museum, Sinsheim
Ju 87B; WNr 1301643; 4./StG 77
On display since 1989, this unrestored Ju 87B of 4.StG 77 was recovered from the sea off St. Tropez. It

was shot down on 16 August 1944, while attacking the Allied invasion of the south of France. The tail unit could not be recovered and is currently lying in 100 metres of water.

Luftfahrttechnisches Museum Rechlin, Germany
This museum has a restored Junkers Ju 87-B1 instrument panel.

Deutsches Technikmuseum Berlin
In 1997 the Museum für Verkehr und Technik in Berlin (now the Deutsches Technikmuseum) bought two Junkers Ju 87s from the New Zealand Fighter Pilots Museum at Wanaka, which specialised in recovering wrecks from north Russia. Both aircraft are largely complete, but have yet to be restored.

Ju 87R-2; w/n 5856; LI+BL
5856 was in service with I/StG 5, and crashed on 2 July 1942 near Murmansk. The aircraft was rescued in 1994.

Ju 87R-4; 6234; L1+FW
C/n 6234 was in service with IV/LG1 (later StG 5) in Russia during WW2. It crashed on 24 April 1942 near Murmansk and was recovered in 1990.

FORMER YUGOSLAVIA
Yugoslav Aeronautical Museum, Belgrade
Ju 87D-2; 0870406 98+01 ex VE+KU
The museum has the tail section of a Ju 87B on display. The centre section, parts of the wings and the engine cowlings are in storage – although recent reports suggest that they may have been sold to a British buyer.

The museum reportedly has parts from three more aircraft in the collection.

BELGIUM
Wreck and parts recovered in Belgium in 1998 and 1999 include parts from several aircraft, including a Ju 87R, W.Nr 5820, formerly flown by SG 102.

Appendix 5
Stuka Models

Three high-quality display Ju 87 kits are available from Aviation-Central.com., as follows:

Ju 87 'Flying Dragon' (1/30th scale).
Order No AERAD-AL, price $209.95

Ju 87 'Afrika Korps' (1/30th scale).
Order No AERAD-AL, price $209.95

Ju 87 'Black Ghost' (1/32nd scale).
Order No AERAD-ST, Price $129.95.

Other models available include:

Corgi:
Ju 87B-2 Stuka (T6+HL of StG 3)

Franklin Mint Armour Collection:
Ju 87B of 6/StG 2 (Flying Snake markings), 1/48th scale

Heller:
Ju 87B-1 (1/72nd scale)

Model Power:
Junkers Ju 87D (1/100 series)

Appendix 6
Stuka Books

Aders, G. and Held, W.
Stuka. Dive Bombers – Pursuit Bombers – Combat Pilots. A Pictorial Chronicle of German Close-Combat Aircraft to 1945.
Schiffer (USA) 1989.

Barker, A.J.
Stuka Ju 87.
Bison Books 1988.

Bateson, Richard P.
Stuka! Junkers Ju 87.
Ducimus Books 1972.

Just, G.
Stuka Pilot Hans-Ulrich Rudel. His Life Story in Words and Photographs.
Schiffer Publishing (USA) 1990.

Nowarra, Heinz J.
Junkers Ju 87: the Stuka Story.
John W. Caler Publications (USA) 1967.

Rudel, Hans-Ulrich
Stuka Pilot.
Euphorion (Ireland) 1952.
(Memoirs of the Luftwaffe's most outstanding ground attack pilot)

Smith, Peter C.
Junkers Ju 87 Stuka.
The Crowood Press 1998.

Smith, Peter C.
Stuka at War.
Ian Allan 1980.

Smith, Peter C.
Stuka Squadron.
PSL 1990.

Vanags-Baginskis, A. and Watanabe, R.
Stuka Ju 87.
Janes Aircraft Spectacular 1982.

List supplied by Frank Smith Maritime & Aviation Books, 100 Heaton Road, Newcastle upon Tyne NE6 5HL. Tel 0191 265 6333

Index

Page numbers in *italics* refer to illustrations.

Africa, North 37-38, *38*, 40, *41*, 48, 50-54, *51*, *52*
Aichi aircraft 7-8
Alamein, Battle of 53
Arado Ar 81: 8-9
armament 69, *72*, *76*, 80, 90, *90*, *91*
    bombs 11, 13, 15, 17, *54*, 69, *72*, *76*, 90, *90*

Balkans campaign 38-39
Blackburn Skua 24-25, *25*
Britain, Battle of 29, 31, 33-34, *33*, 35, 36, 65
Bruck, *Oberst* Helmut 63, 64
Bulgarian Air Force, Royal 58, *60*

Clarke, Squadron Leader D.H. 83-84
cockpit 15
construction 14-15
Crete 40, 42, 44
Curtiss XF11C-2 Goshawk 6-7

de Gaulle, Colonel Charles 28
diving 82-83
Dunkirk 30-32

Eastern Front 54-59, *55*, *56*, *57*, *58*, *59*, 60, 62-63, 68, 84-86
    see also Operation *Barbarossa*
Enneccerus, *Generalmajor* Walter 64
Erfurth, Kurt 62

Fieseler Fi 98A 10
flying the Ju 87: 81-84
France, Battle of, 1940 27-33, 66

Gasmann, *Major* Peter 64
German Army, Grossdeutschland division 57-58
Goering, Hermann 6-7
Gorovets, Lieutenant A.K. 56
Graf Zeppelin (aircraft carrier) 17, 20, 21, 64, 72
Greece 39, *43*, 44
ground strafing 84-85

Hagen, *Generalleutnant* Walter 64, *64*
Hamburger Ha 137 (formerly P.6) 8, 9-10, *10*
Heinkel He 50: 7, 8, 11
Heinkel He 118: 8, 10, 11, *11*
Henschel Hs 123: 10-11
Henschel Hs 126: 28
Hozzel, *Hauptmann* Paul-Werner 24, 64-65
Hull, Flight Lieutenant Caesar 25, 27
Hungarian Air Force, Royal 58, 84-86, *85*

Italian air force (*Regia Aeronautica*) 37, 47, 48, *48*, 53

Junkers, Hugo 5, 6, 10, 61, *61*, 62
Junkers Flugzeugwerke AG 17
    CL.1: 5
    F.13 (formerly J.13) 6, 61
    G.24: *7*, 62
    G.38: *8*, 62
    Ju 52 and Ju 52/3m 6, 9, *22*, 62
    Ju 87 Stuka 40, *43*, *51*, *53*, *58*, *60*, *82*, *83*, 88, *90*; formations *22*, *59*, *87*; StG 2: *45*, *55*
    Ju 87A 69, *72*; Ju 87A-0: 13, 69; Ju 87A-1: 13, *15*, *16*, 69; Ju 87A-2: 13, 69
    Ju 87B 13-14, *17*, *17*, 20, 24, *35*, 45, 49, *52*, 88, *90*; early production *16*; LG 1: *29*; Spain *20*; 7./StG 1: *31*; StG 2: *26*, *49*; T6+HL *33*; TD+AY *27*; Ju 87B-1: *17*, *23*, *65*, *66*, 69, *72*, *73*; Ju 87B-1 (Trop) *47*, *48*; Ju 87B-2: *17*, *36*, *46*, *72*
    Ju 87C *17*, 20, 72
    Ju 87D *54*, 67, *68*, *73*, *76*, *76*; Ju 87D-1: *73*, *76*; Ju 87D-1 (Trop) *77*; Ju 87D-2: *76*; Ju 87D-3: *50*, *56*, *76*, *77*; Ju 87D-4: *76*; Ju 87D-5: *56*, *60*, 80, 84, *85*; Ju 87D-6/-7/-8: 80
    Ju 87E/F 80
    Ju 87G *56*, 62-63, 80; Ju 87G-1: *57*, 80, *90*; Ju 87G-2: 80
    Ju 87H 80-81, *81*

Ju 87K 81
Ju 87R 24, 25; Ju 87R-1: *44*, 72-73; Ju 87R-2 (Trop) 73; Ju 87R-4: 73
Ju 87V-1 (prototype) 8, 10, 11, *12*, 62; Ju 87V-2: 11, 13, *13*, 62; Ju 87V-3: 13, *14*; Ju 87V-4: 13
K47: 5-6, 62
W.33: 6, 61

Kursk, Battle of 56-58, 63

landing 83, *83*
Lang, *Hauptmann* Friedrich 65-66, *65*
Levay, Gyozo 84-86
Luftwaffe
    II Fliegerkorps 34, 48
    VIII *Fliegerkorps* 27, 29, 30, 31-32, 33, 39, 45, 55, 67-68
    IV(Stuka)/LG (*Lehrgeschwader*) 1: *29*, 33, 34, 44, 54
    StG (*Stukageschwader*) 1: 24, 25, 30, 33-34, 37, 54-55, 64, 86; I/StG 1: 24, 65; II/StG 1: 34, 44, 45; III/StG 1: 21, 34, 44, 45; 7./StG 1: 31, 67
    StG 2: 21, 26, 30, 36, 40, 42, 45, 55, 56, 86-87; I/StG 2: 42, 44, 45, 49, 55; II/StG 2: 45, 64; III/StG 2: 33, 44, 45, 46; IV/StG 2: 36
    StG 3: 34, 54, 56, 87, 88; III/StG 3: 50, 51
    StG 5: 56, 87-88; I/StG 5 (formerly IV(Stuka)/LG 1) 54
    StG 51: 33, 88
    StG 76: 88; I/StG 76: 20, 22
    StG 77: 30, 34, 36, 44, 45-46, 56, 88
    I/StG 162 'Immelmann' 11, 13
    I/StG 186: 32
    IV/StG 186: 21
    4.(Stuka)/186: 20, 72
    ZG 26 'Horst Wessel' 41
Lydekker, Lieutenant Antony 25, 27

Malta 37, 39, 40, *40*, *41*, 48, 51, 52
Messerschmitt Bf 110: *41*

Neuenhofen, Willy 62
night operations 59
Norway 24, 25, *25*, 27

Operation *Barbarossa* 44-46, *45*, 48
Operation *Battleaxe* 50
Operation *Citadel* 57
Operation *Crusader* 50

Peel, Squadron Leader J.R.A. 34
Pohlmann, Dipl-Ing Hermann 8, 62
Poland 21-22, *22*, 24
powerplant 15
Pressler, *Oberstleutnant* Gustav 67

Richthofen, *Major* (later *Generalfeldmarschall*) Wolfram Freiherr von 8, 13, 27, 30, 59, 67-68
Romanian Air Force, Royal 58
Royal Air Force: No 73 Squadron *38*; No 213 Squadron *50*
Rudel, *Leutnant* (later *Oberstleutnant*) Hans-Ulrich 46, 56, 58, 62-63, *63*

Schwarzkopff, *Oberst* Gunter 68
shipping attacks 21, 24, 46, 62
    British 24, 25, 27, 33, 37, 40, 42, 44, 51, 52
Sicily *49*
Spanish Civil War (Condor Legion) 10, 13, 17, *20*, 67
Stalingrad 55

tail unit construction 15
take-off 81-82
Tobruk 37-38, 50-51, 52-53

Udet, Ernst 6, *6*, 7, 10, 11

Versailles, Treaty of 5, 6, 61
Vickers Wellington 39

wing construction 14-15

Zemsky, *Hauptmann* Johan 68